The Kaldewey Press, New York

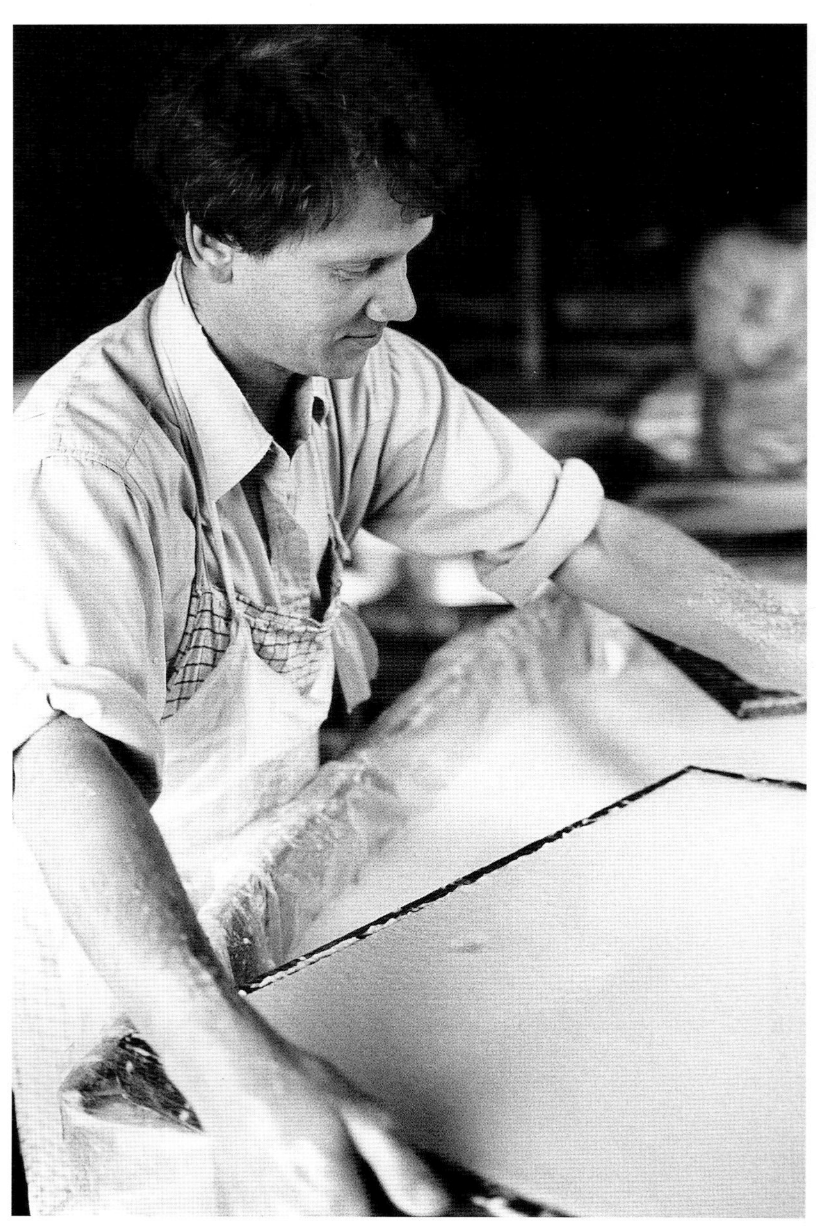

Gunnar A. Kaldewey

Crossing Borders

The Kaldewey Press, New York

Mindell Dubansky

and Monica J. Strauss

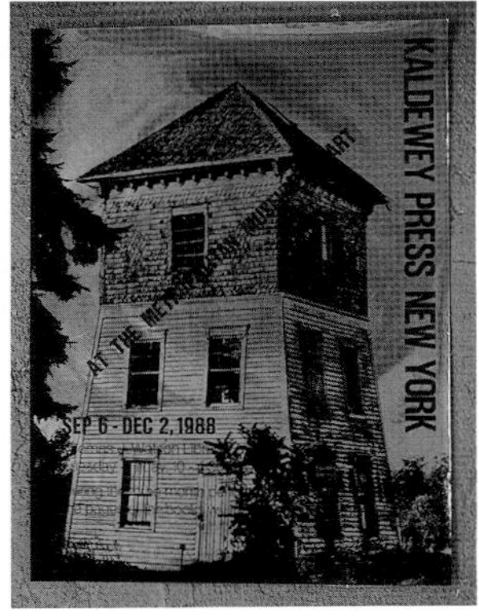

Cantz

Contents

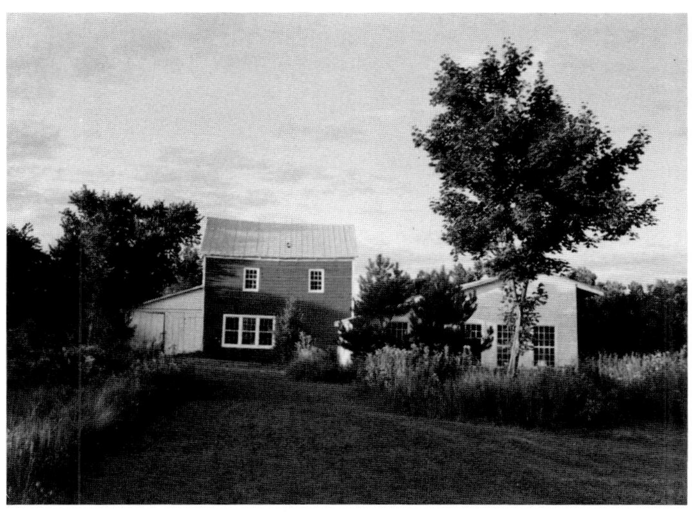

Printshop and Studio in Poestenkill, New York

Preface

To make a picture is one thing, to make a so-called artists' book another. The things are simply completely different.

The independent picture forces one to bundle together objects of interest according to the principal of simultaneity and eventually place them in the picture in this way. Everything is present at the same time – there is no *before*, there is no *after*. This means that the independent picture cannot take up or transmit certain things of interest.

The fact of paging through a book permits another approach. Suddenly there is a *before* and there is an *after*, there is the factor of time, there is a sequence of pictures that permit aspects to be integrated that the independent picture cannot take up. Also there is the additional opportunity to work with a text, a possibility that is always difficult when it comes to the independent picture.

Above all after completing a certain series of group of pictures, it seems to me that making a book offers the welcome chance to reorder the objects of interest and the picture in a new or different way. Every created order is temporary and only by not accepting preordained and even self-created order, does the desire for disorder and a re-ordering occur. Things that might be rejected in connection with the individual picture, now appear in a new context, in a new order and on the basis of the formal peculiarity of the book can suddenly be meaningful. Precisely this re-working of rejected materials, sketches, and ideas is a decisive aspect for me.

Many things that never come up in the independent picture, come up in books. Some pictures require *before*-images and sometimes also *after*-images.

Monica J. Strauss

Crossing Borders – The Kaldewey Press, New York

A summer spent collaborating on a limited-edition book with Gunnar Kaldewey in the rural setting of his Kaldewey Press in Poestenkill, New York, gave rise to the reflections on the opposite page by the German artist Heribert Ottersbach. For years the two had planned to do a book together, but it was not until Kaldewey discovered a text seemingly tailor-made for Ottersbach's obsession with the visual vocabulary of disaster, that the match was joined. The result was Edition Kaldewey No. 20., Walter Benjamin's *Angelus Novus, Über den Begriff der Geschichte* (Angelus Novus, On the Concept of History, 1993) (see page 7 + 39). Benjamin's vision of the angel of history turning toward the past where catastrophe piles "wreckage upon wreckage" was a pessimistic one and Otterbach's veiled images drawn from the news media proved to be a telling accompaniment. With this opportunity to make a book on his own artistic terms, Ottersbach joined the ranks of at least sixteen other contemporary artists from several countries invited to work at the Kaldewey Press since 1980.

Gunnar Kaldewey began his career as a prodigy in a field in where age and experience usually count for more than youth. From childhood, books had been his passion and by twenty-nine, he was one of the youngest and most successful antiquarian book dealers in Germany with an unerring nose for the rarest items in his field of eighteenth-century literature. It was his flair for marketing those discoveries through innovative catalogues that gradually pointed him in a new direction. Kaldewey began to see that he was far more absorbed in the process of creating these publications, than acquiring the books they described.

The catalogues were printed at the Waldkircher Verlagsgesellschaft in the Black Forest, and it was there that two of the letterpress printers – Klaus Bühler and Heinrich Lehmann – taught Kaldewey the trade. Under their tutelage, Kaldewey made his first book in 1976: A slim, elegant keepsake volume in an edition of 30 copies it was intended for fellow members of an all-male cooking club. *Grimod de la Renière* (see page 7 + 45) an essay by Franz Blei, dealt with a well-born, one-armed eighteenth-century French gourmand who took pride in the advantage his iron limb gave him in handling hot pots and cauldrons. In this initial effort, Kaldewey's typography was sober and traditional, but in combining rich materials with a simple presentation – yellow Japanese paper bound between, light and unusually flexible embossed black boards by the Hamburg binder Christian Zwang – he had the beginning of the style that would distinguish his brand of artist's books. The printing of *Grimod de la Renière* ignited Kaldewey's creativity in a way that selling never had and, ultimately, it led the way to the Kaldewey Press editions, the imprint for his own artistic ventures.

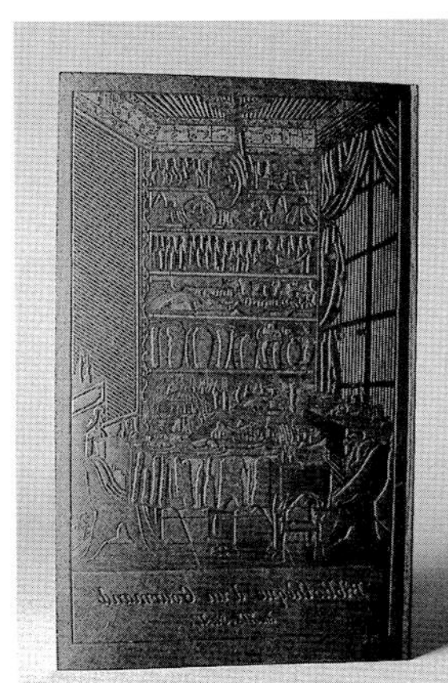

If 1976 marked the year of Kaldewey's debut as an artist-printer, but still left him straddling the two worlds of the eighteenth and twentieth centuries, 1977 pushed him over the edge into his own time. This was the year of his first visit to New York after long resisting the pull of the great metropolis and it made of him an immediate convert to the cosmopolitan way of life. On returning to Hamburg from his three-month stay, Kaldewey immediately set

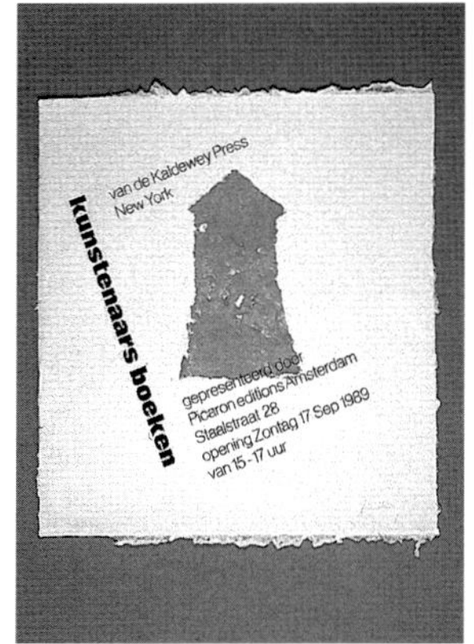

A

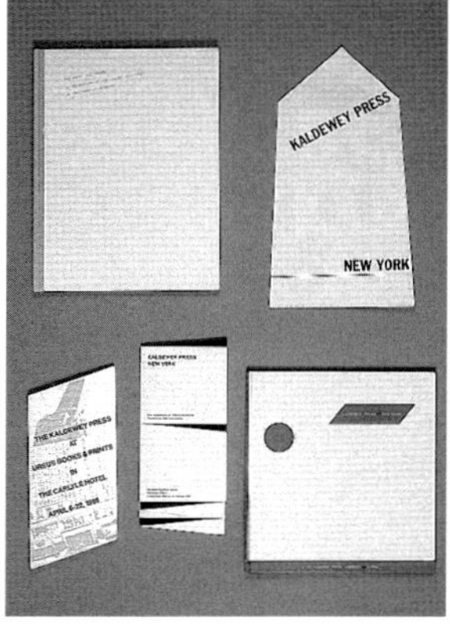

B

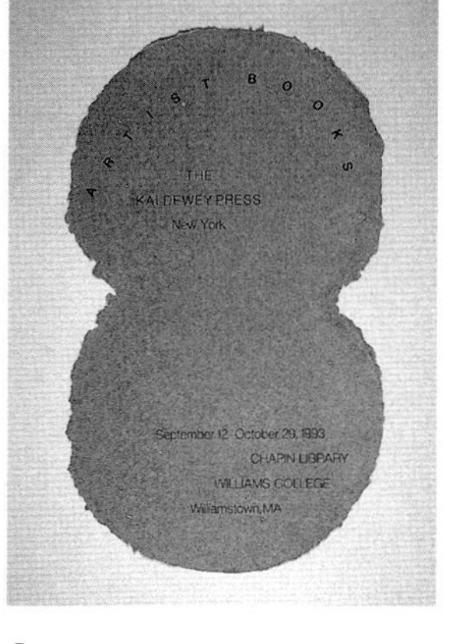

C

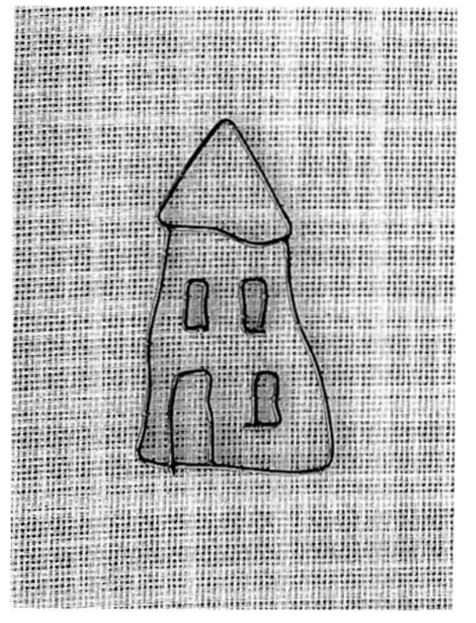

D

to work on *New York 1977* (**see page 46, 47 + 93**), his second book and a joyful assent not only to the experience of the city but to modern life. A subway token embedded in the cover introduced the reader to the wide diversity of images and ephemera – high-minded and low – that were flung across sixty pages of free-wheeling typography. The exuberant text captured the hub-bub, the sensory overload, the sheer exaltation of the newcomer mastering a great and complex city for the first time.

A second consequence of Kaldewey's introduction to the new world was an intense desire to initiate a dialogue with American artists of his own gener-ation. Drawing upon the entrepreneurial style that had marked his early suc-cess, he took the initiative of inviting young American artists to Germany, putting them up at his new Düsseldorf home and arranging small exhibitions of their work in his bookshop/gallery. In return, he asked only that they join him in producing a book. This was the spontaneous beginning of Kaldewey's second imprint, Kaldewey Editions, dedicated to creative collaborations with artists of his own generation.

Gradually book dealing was supplanted by Kaldewey's increasing commit-ment to printing and publishing and by 1985, newly settled in America, the transition was complete. Having acquired a commodious nineteenth-century country estate in the rural upstate New York town of Poestenkill, he set up a home for the Kaldewey-Press. Outbuildings on the property became paper-making facilities and studios and with the exception of the bindings, every aspect of the books could be made here. The water tower with its pitched roof and distinctive angled walls became the Press's symbol (**see fig. A–C**) and is used as logo, watermark (**see fig. D**), and vignette in the books. Over the years, through the network of letterpress print enthusiasts all over the coun-try, type and a variety of presses have been acquired for printing. On hand today are two Van der Cook proof-presses – one from the 1930's and another – among the last to be produced by the company – made in the 1960's. The latter is Kaldewey's personal "work horse" and since he found it in a Boston newspaper shop under a photograph of a political hero of his youth, John F. Kennedy, he feels a symbolic bond. The artists also have at their disposal a Fuchs & Lange lithography press that originally belonged to the Tamarind Press and came to Poestenkill (with the lithographic stones) via the University of Santa Barbara, and an elegant Etan etching press with elliptical cylinders.

In Poestenkill, the pattern of hospitality first established in Germany, has become a way of life. Every summer two books are produced there – one written, illustrated, and printed by Kaldewey, himself, the other a collabora-tive effort with a visiting artist from the U.S., Europe or Asia. Projects gener-ally take two years from the time Kaldewey and the artist agree on a text to the delivery of the books from the binder. In the autumn, when the previous season's work is concluded, the paper for the next year's publications is made. By the following summer, the paper, no longer "green," is ready for printing and the artist comes to stay in the Poestenkill compound. The books evolve in the studio and press room as artist and printer work together and independently. If all goes well, the pages are ready to go off to the binder in the fall and by that time the sharing of summer pleasures, much good food and an abundance of wine has firmly integrated art and life.

All the books produced by the Kaldewey Press are generous in format and have an average print run of not more – and often less – than sixty copies. Most of them are printed letterpress, a method Kaldewey finds both aesthetically satisfying and efficient for small editions that undergo many transformations before completion. Publication is usually in two editions – regular and deluxe – but sometimes a "third" or "special edition" is included with a different kind of paper. The de luxe editions may include a separate suite of illustrations, hand-coloring, or fine papers, but their mark of distinction is their creative and expressive bindings.

The winter months, when the Press has its headquarters in New York City, are dedicated to exhibitions and lectures. Since its inception, the Kaldewey Press has had more than fifty exhibitions in bookstores, libraries, galleries and museums in America and Europe. In the U.S.A., Kaldewey's books have been on display, among other places, in the Metropolitan Museum of Art, New York, the Getty Center, Santa Monica, California, the Houghton Library, Harvard University, Cambridge, Massachusetts and Williams College, Williamstown, Massachusetts. Some of the venues in which Kaldewey books have been shown in Europe are the Galerie Yvon Lambert, Paris; Galerie Niepel, Düsseldorf; Kunstklubben, Oslo; Deutsche Bücherei, Leipzig; and the Irish Museum of Modern Art, Dublin.

The dialogue between the artist and the book has been a particularly fruitful one in the 20th century and in launching his press, Kaldewey joined a long tradition of bibliophilic entrepreneurs who have made it possible. Like the French publishers of the classic livre d'artiste such as Vollard and Teriade, Kaldewey functions as an impresario, inviting the artists, funding the materials and printing, and personally promoting and marketing the books. The generous formats of the Kaldewey productions, and their elegant (but decidedly contemporary) bindings also have their source in his great French predecessors. But as a printer and an artist, Kaldewey has a closer kinship with the members of early 20th-century Russian avant-garde. Those artists created and often printed their own books, challenging every received notion of what materials, typography, illustrations and, even content, were appropriate for the form.

The two traditions – French and Russian – can be said to have come together in the books made by the writer/printer/publisher Ilya Zdanevich, known as Iliazd, in Paris after World War II. As a member of the Russian avant-garde in Tiflis at the time of the Revolution, Zdanevich produced surprising books in which the free play of the typography became an art form in itself. After settling in Paris in the twenties, his printing experiments bore further fruit in his designs for Dada ephemera and posters. Eager to remind a new generation of the typographic achievements of his youth, Iliazd began to publish a series of livres d'artiste in the late 1940's, in which printer and artist shared equally in the creative challenge of each volume. As a result the books he made with Picasso, Miró, Giacometti, and, particularly, Max Ernst resulted in new departures for the form and it is from this tradition that the Kaldewey press stems.

Having mapped some of the precedents for Kaldewey's work, it must be said that the profile of the Kaldewey Press with its emphasis on the personal, the contemporary, and the international is very much Gunnar Kaldewey's own and differentiates him from both his predecessors and his colleagues in today's world of limited-edition publishing. The artistic impulses behind the Kaldewey Press are either those of Kaldewey, himself, or an artist of his generation. The books, although very different from one another, share a modernist aesthetic, and the texts – mutually agreed upon by artist and publisher – are always significant works drawn from a wide range of languages and cultures.

The Kaldewey Press Imprint

Books published under the Kaldewey Press imprint are made by Kaldewey himself as writer, printer, and artist. The key to them all is the personal response, even if it is never again as overt as *New York 1977* (Kaldewey Press 1, 1978). Starting out with the expression of a psyche, Kaldewey Press books move toward the adventure of a mind. Their mix of intellectual, poetic, and visual reflections on the works of man and nature in the course of a peripatetic life parallel aspects of publications by Joseph Beuys and Richard Long. Like them, Kaldewey has the reader draw on senses beyond the visual and the tactility of sand, the fragrance of wood, the recorded sounds of the desert at night might be part of the experience of the book.

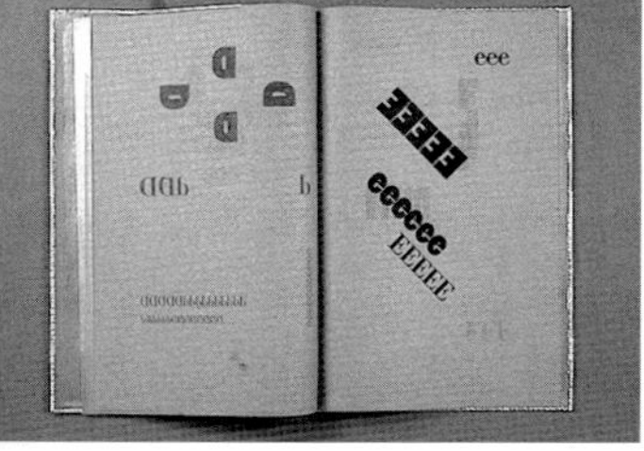

Some of the early productions are self-reflective – they explore the life of the press. *ABC* (Kaldewey Press 3, 1983) **(see page 10 + 95)**; for instance, celebrates the new world of letterforms. In this very unorthodox alphabet, display types wheel, dance, and somersault across colored papers, sometimes with an illicit partner from further down the alphabetic line. Endpapers sprayed with car paint salute the printer's new American environment. *Images* (Kaldewey Press 4, 1986) **(see page 50 + 96)**, the first book with paper made by Kaldewey, himself, documents his apprenticeship in papermaking in Aspen, Colorado, under the supervision of Margaret Prentice, one of the founders of Twinrocker Paper. After years of negotiating with the late Shusaku Tomi, the famous paper-maker in Wajima, Japan, Kaldewey finally received – in two wooden boxes – 1000 sheets of his sukigawa-gama paper made of cedar bark. The acquisition of this extraordinary paper, the texture of which seemed closer to some organic growth than anything made by man, inspired *Trees* (Kaldewey Press 6, 1988) **(see page 10, 52, 53 + 98)**, a poetic salute to the leafy denizens of Poestenkill.

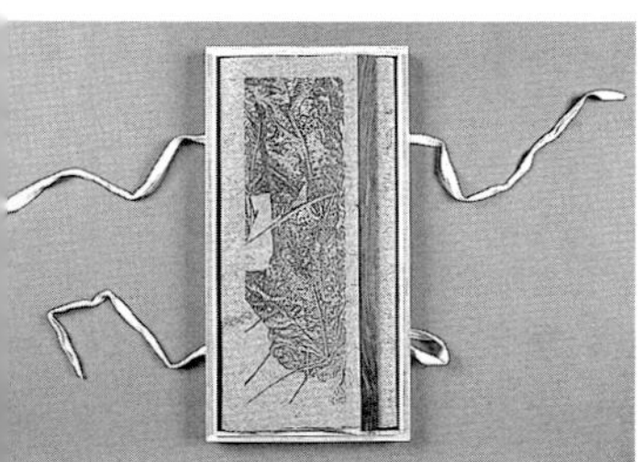

In 1990 Kaldewey produced *Books as Art, A Lecture* (Kaldewey Press 8) **(see page 55 + 100)**, an eloquent statement of the Press's credo after several years of publishing. "It is curiosity about a new text that inspires me to find a new form," he wrote. "It encourages me to take risks again and again, to find new ways in the use of materials, and new conceptions for the aesthetic of the book."

A second group of Kaldewey Press books examines the history and lore of personally meaningful places. In these books, Kaldewey mingles the sublime and the factual – poetry, description, and statistics – to suggest how we make the inanimate our own. The two volumes that make up *Changing Waters*

(Kaldewey Press Editions # 9 and # 10) (see page 56 + 57) are dedicated to the Hudson and the Rhine, rivers that ran past Kaldewey's homes in New York and Düsseldorf. The elongated horizontal format of the covers bound in light and dark green leathers, respectively, contain ten and eleven-meter fold-outs – the page as river. The Hudson volume is lighter in tone, reflecting the far shorter and less complicated recorded history of the region. Blue and black droplets run between the poetic texts of the Indians – who called the Hudson "Lake Tear of the Clouds" – and the Dutch explorers. Gradually, poetry is replaced by the words of our mundane reality as awe in the face of nature is replaced by its abuse.

Turning to the Rhine in Volume 2 (see page 57), Kaldewey conveys the far greater density of history and culture on its banks. Visually, the image of the river is less sprightly than that of the Hudson. Its stolid flow is indicated by an elongated rectangular shape repeated on every page. Variations of current, weather, depth – even pollution – are suggested by subtle shifts of blues, greens, yellows, and browns. There is repetition, also, in a laconic, factual description which appears on every other page in one of the six languages spoken along the river's course – Romantsch, Switzerdütsch, French, German, English, and Dutch. In contrast are the quotations from the many poets who have been moved to eloquence by the river's beauty. These range from medieval Gottfried von Strassburg (1215) to the modern Marcel Broodthaers (1975). An all-white embossed double-page spread at the center of the volume enshrines two of the most famous hommages to the river – Byron's *Childe Harold's Pilgrimage* (1818) and Heinrich Heine's *Die Lorelei* (1827), bringing home the Romantic poets' passion for nature. In contrast is the modern elegy that closes the book – but it is not poetry. It reads Ciba-Geigy, Basel; Bayer, Leverkusen; Mannesmann, Düsseldorf; Thyssen, Duisburg; Krupp, Essen.

Kaldewey Press 11, *Asia, America, Europe* (1944) (see page 101) the most recent effort in the series, takes on the three continents by examining three representative buildings – the Cathedral of Cologne in Germany, the World Trade Center in the U.S.A., and the Longhua Pagoda in China. They are expressions, too, of the layers of culture, most meaningful to Kaldewey himself – his German origins, his passion for the New World, and his partner in life, the Chinese composer Bun Ching Lam. The three structures, all famous for their heights but so different in form and so different in meaning are silkscreened from Kaldewey's photo-collages onto three separate Mylar scrolls. Printed in white on a translucent medium, they lose their materiality and dissolve into the symbols they have become of three different approaches to life. The accompanying booklets are printed on the same material with details from the larger images, but descriptions differ with each monument and continent. The Pagoda is seen as an accumulation of poetic architectural details – pavilions, balustrades, verandas, disks on golden chains – all intended to enhance Buddhist meditation. The World Trade Center is described as a compendium of statistics – 43,600 windows, 12 million square feet of rental space, 110 floors, 239 elevators, etc. In contrast the story of Cathedral of Cologne emphasizes tales of survival.

Leaving the earth behind, *Light Years* (Kaldewey Press 12, 1996) propels the reader into the expanded cosmos revealed by modern technology. The beauty of the photographs taken by the Hubble Telescope inspired Kaldewey to draw upon them for a series of double-spread collages to accompany descriptions of our changing conceptions of the universe (see page 102). Printed from metal cuts in a rich range of colors on large, damp sheets, the collages take on the appearance of etchings. They allow the reader's fantasy to take flight as he contemplates texts touching on such imponderables as the drifting of 50 billion galaxies or the existence of 43 other solar systems that resemble our own. The anchoring of the cosmos by the activity of the mind is reflected in further pages studded with the names of the stars of the Northern and Southern hemispheres. But it is the romance of the heavens that is found on the supple, dove-grey leather binding embossed with bursts of silver starlight (see fig. 109).

The Edition Kaldewey Imprint

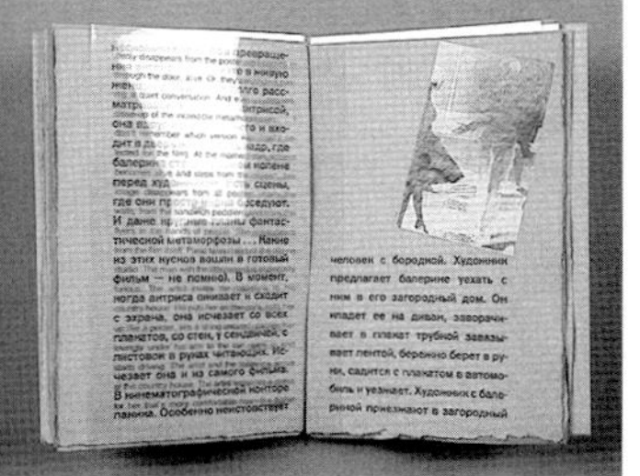

Twenty-six Kaldewey Editions have been published till now and each one represents a contemporary artist's dialogue with a chosen text in its original tongue. The writers include the great modernists – Joyce, Beckett, Yeats, Mayakovsky (see page 12 + 26), Kafka and Neruda – representatives of the post-modern stream – Duras, Burroughs (see page 12, 23, 71 + 72), Pasolini, Ashbery (see page 32 + 88), Caponegro, Celan, and Benjamin – and a few challenging classics – Confucius, Ovid, the Hebrew poet of the Song of Songs and Kleist. As the impresario of these projects, Kaldewey starts out coaching on the sidelines encouraging his collaborators to experiment freely with their chosen media, whether it is photography or Xerox; lithography, etching or woodcut; paper pulp or paper cutouts; transparent, translucent, or folded and cut pages. As a printer and an artist, himself, he invites the challenge to his skill as a press man. Since his vision of the contemporary book is the integration of image and text, the joining of the veral and the visual impulse must constantly be re-negotiated. What makes him successful in this regard, amid the strong artistic personalities that he chooses as his collaborators, is the minimalist aesthetic that governs his approach to printing and bookmaking. With Helvetica as his typeface of choice and a penchant for a clear, legible and spacious presentation of the text, he provides the matrix that keeps artist and writer in balance.

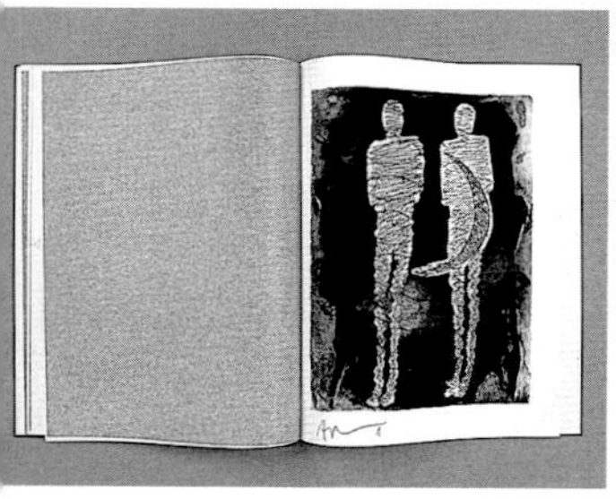

The first books of the Edition Kaldewey, which bear the imprint Düsseldorf/New York represent the experimental period of the Press. Some publications are purely visual, in others artist and writer are one and the same, a few mark the first attempts at matching text and artist. The imagery ranges from color photography (*New York Reflections,* 1980 (see page 21), and *New York Reflections Two,* 1983, Kaldewey Editions 1 and 6) to original pencil drawings (Everett Potter, *Cave Pictures,* drawing by Jonathan Lasker, 1981, Kaldewey Edition 2) (see page 22) to the tour de force cutouts, color xeroxes, stamps and collage that expressed the rich fantasy life of the late John Eric Broaddus (*Sphinx and the Bird of Paradise,* 1981, Kaldewey Edition 3) (see page 69). Broaddus, in fact, decked himself out in a similar manner shocking Kaldewey's conservative neighbors in Düsseldorf.

One of the most interesting productions of this period and a harbinger of things to come is the first book by the Japanese sculptor Jun Suzuki. *In the Beginning* (Kaldewey Edition 7, 1984) (see page 24 + 25) is comprised of 12 metal sheets, each of which displays a Japanese word silkscreened in red, with its English equivalent in perforated stencils below. The words chosen – "breath," "scream," "listen," "growl," etc., are intended to illustrate the process of the creation of language. On the last page, the first sentence of the earliest known work of Japanese literature appears in original brushwork and letterpress on Japanese paper. From this time on, several of Kaldewey's projects will explore the expressive quality of letterforms in their many linguistic and written guises. They will also use materials as metaphors for a book's meaning. In Suzuki's book the metal alludes, first of all, to the artist's usual medium – the materials of sculpture. But its use also refers back to earlier experiments with the book form. The Italian Futurist artists created metal books in an attempt to subvent traditional expectations. In Suzuki's version, the weight and density of the pages is the antithesis of the subject – language, all breath and air. It is only when language achieves its own permanence in writing, that the artist resorts to paper.

Because each collaboration has its own dynamic, it is difficult to categorize the Kaldewey Editions that followed these first efforts. For the sake of clarity, however, and with a few exceptions, it is possible to discuss them in three categories of emphasis – books in which the material sets the tone, books where form is the vehicle, and books that focus on variations of the written word.

For Kaldewey and some of his collaborators, paper is a medium with great expressive possibilities. The first demonstration of this is one of Kaldewey's most imaginative projects dedicated to Paul Celan's cycle of poems *Mohn und Gedächtnis (Poppy Seeds and Memory)*, written in 1952. The intensity of the verses which allude to the poet's experience of the Holocaust suggested to Kaldewey that they should be absorbed and interpreted over time. For that reason he asked the young 23-year-old German conceptual artist Mischa Kuball to collaborate with him on three separate publications to be done at five-year intervals. The first of these was *Todesfuge* (Kaldewey Edition 9, 1984) (see page 27 + 73), the last part of the cycle, but the most well known. The rhythms and repetitions of these verses are as haunting as the metaphors. Color and substance belong to the captor alone. The victims partake of absence – "black milk," ashes, smoke, and air. Kuball's visual response honors the victims in kind with a series of austere and elegiac paper cuts on heavy white Fabriano stock. Each treated sheet has a life of its own as the fragments open with the turning of the page and the void thus exposed speaks.

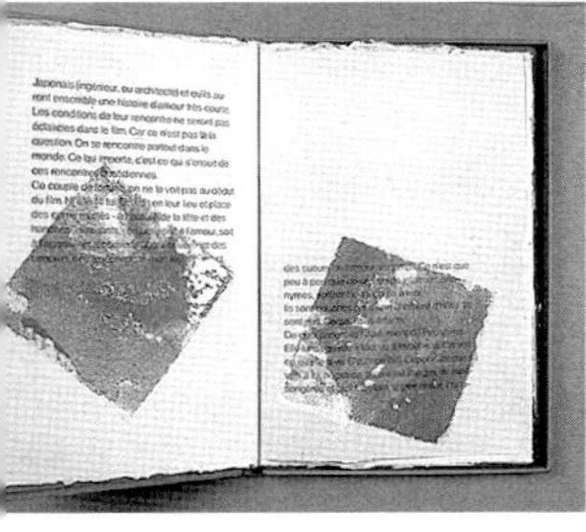

... Kaldewey Edition 10, *Hiroshima Mon Amour: A Synopsis* by Marguerite Duras, 1985–1986 (see page 13, 28, 74 + 75), was the American sculptor Ann Sperry's debut as a book artist. The text is more than a summary of the author's film made in 1958, it is a literary exegesis explaining the underlying symbolic structure of the screenplay. In recounting the short-lived affair between a French actress and a Japanese architect in Hiroshima thirteen years after the bombing, Duras uses eroticism to explore its opposite coin – the degrading intimacies of war. Both lovers are marked by their experiences during the last days of World War II. He is pursued by memories of the atomic bomb, she cannot forget the murder of her German lover and the humiliation of being accused and punished as a collaborator.

The text is printed on folio-sized, deckle-edged sheets of brilliant pink. Embedded in the pages are Sperry's paper-pulp images done in shades of rose, flame, and charcoal gray.

These semi-abstract phallic and female images blossom form the margins of the initial pages, undergo several metamorphoses throughout the book, and are finally transformed into suggestions of weapons, fire, and destruction. A second expressive device is the use of folded sheets with tissue-thin edges reminiscent of flame and charring. At the center of the book, the sequence of pages is abruptly broken by the appearence of such a sheet in black. When opened, it reveals the pathetic recounting of the actress's experiences.

For Sperry, the opportunity of working with the medium of paper-pulp, opened new expressive possibilities:

Distant images, remembrances of the powerfully erotic opening of the film, were the inspiration to make a paper for this book that would become a symbol of flesh – not any one person's skin, but a sensuous surface and color that would evoke these feelings… The actual making of the paper – Gunnar pulling each fresh sheet from the vat, and my placing the shimmering colored paper-pulp images on those fleshy surfaces – remains one of my most fulfilling artistic experiences.

The language, the colors, the materials of an artist's homeland, make up the weave of *Ciant da li campanis, Poesias rumantschas, cun disegns da Not Vital (Song of the Bells, Romantsch Poems with Drawings by Not Vital,* Kaldewey Edition 12, 1988) (see page 14, 30, 31, 78 + 79). Much of Not Vital's art is inspired by his native corner of Switzerland, the mountain village of Sent in the Lower Engadine, a region distinguished by the local language of Romantsch. In this book Vital celebrates two Romantsch poets – Luisa Famos and Andri Peer – and pays hommage to a third, Pier Paolo Pasolini, who sometimes wrote verse in Friulian, a dialect close to Vital's own.

At the heart of this book, too, is the very special and rare sugikawa-gami paper, made by Shusaku Tomi. The three versions of the book use different variations of this paper. The regular edition of loose pages in a wooden box is divided between twenty-five copies on light brown paper and twenty-five on dark. After this version was completed, the remaining untrimmed sheets of the paper retained such a powerful presence that the artist and printer made the audacious decision to print an "elephant folio" version of ten copies. The size was determined by the full extent of the paper with its deckled edges (see page 14, 30 + 79).

Opening this huge volume – 100 x 64 cm – with its rough-hewn covers of untreated Russian birch and massive, crude creaking hinges is like entering a barn. And inside, nothing interferes with the monumental impression of the paper which is clamped in place by a simple steel rod that leaves all four edges revealed. Vital's gestural acts of charring, ripping, and dabbing with paint distresses further the rough texture of the mud-colored pages and the addition of collage elements of black duck tape and serrated saw blades sug-

14

gest all the bleakness of country life in winter. The poems, printed on separate sheets of thin paper, are pasted in, but the notations on title, contents, and colophon pages are written with the same black crayon Vital uses for his images. Like them, they resemble random markings about to be washed away in the next siege of inclement weather. The entire production is imbued with the sentiment of the last line of Pasolini's poem: *Straniero, al mio dolce volo per piano non aver paura; io sono uno spirito d'amore. Che al suo paese torna di lontana.*

Many of the Kaldewey Editions have unusual configurations designed to express some aspect of the texts they contain. One of the first of these was Kaldewey Edition 11, 1986, the triangular shaped *Quatre Poèmes/Four Songs* by Samuel Beckett with six etchings and the poems set to music (on an enclosed recording) by the composer Bun Ching Lam (see page 29, 76 + 77). Although the poems were not written as a suite – *Dieppe* appeared in 1937, the other three in 1948 – they share the theme of existential isolation. These are not laments, however, the indifference of the cosmos is seen as a source of comfort amid "the panting, the frenzies towards succour towards love."

The economy of Beckett's verse is well served by the geometric crispness of the triangular form. The wide, tapering sheets allow the longer lines to unroll on the page and provide a format for a variety of layouts that visually link the French and English version or give expressive emphasis to the meaning of the poems. A real printing tour de force is the handling of the third poem *"Que ferais je"* where both the second half of the purple-inked French verse and the entire green-inked English version are set at acute angles to one another paralleling the form of the triangular sheet. But instead of creating an easy symmetry, the English poem crosses the center fold halfway down the page and invades the space of its French counterpart. Lam's green-inked etchings are made up of scraps of musical notations and snatches of song. Scattered in an almost arbitrary manner throughout the work, they are an imaginative reflection of both the sense of dislocation in the poems and their stoic wit. They also point to the particular rhythm of her songs.

Kaldewey found the solution for his planned publication of Pablo Neruda's *20 poemas de amour y una cancion desesperada (20 Love Poems and One Song of Despair)* (Kaldewey Edition 15, 1989) (see page 34 + 83) in a weekly calendar designed by Herbert Bayer. The Bauhaus designer had extended the page for each week a little beyond the one before thereby making the sequence visible and accessible at every juncture. Kaldewey recognized that Neruda's numerical title could also be read as a calendar referring as it does to the cycle of a love affair in its inevitable progression from passion to loss. The graduated sizes of the pages would reflect the course of love from the first brief moment of attraction, through the deepening of affection over time, to the last and longest stretch of memory. His adaption of Bayer's concept made for one of the most astonishing first pages in the publisher's œuvre. There, at one glance is the title page, table of contents, and, indeed, the book in its entirety, and yet the secrets of the hot-blooded imagery of Neruda's poems and Kim Keever's colored linoleum cuts lie hidden behind the serene march of letters and numbers across a wide expanse of unadorned pages in echelon.

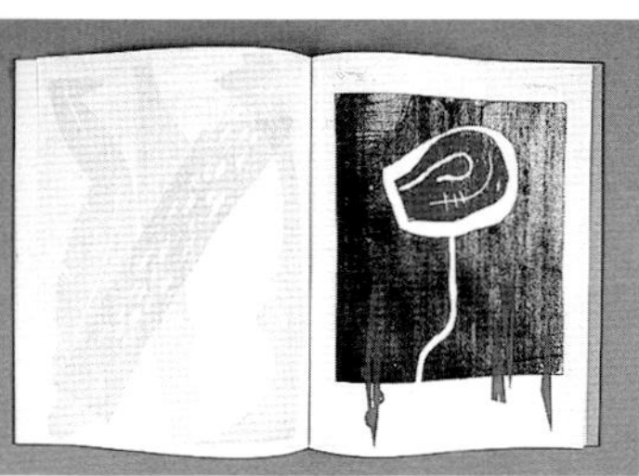

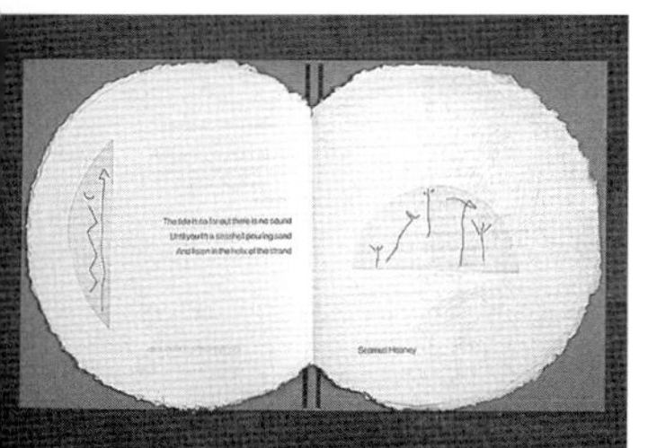

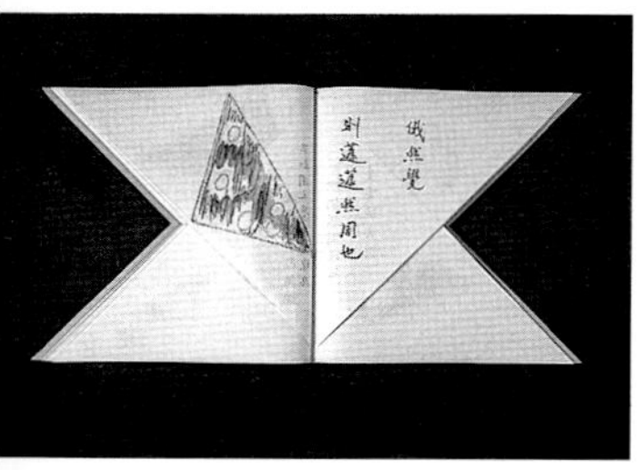

The graduated sizes of the 120 pages also gave Keever's symbolic male and female forms – restricted at first to the narrow confines of the initial sheets – a chance to grow in space and meaning. As each poem has its own title in the written sequence and yet remains connected to the whole, so each image combines motifs relating both to the specific poem on the page and to what has gone before.

Subject and form are more literally joined in two recent Kaldewey Editions. *Sandymount Strand* (Kaldewey Edition 21, 1993) and Chuang Tsu, *Dream of a Butterfly* (Kaldewey Edition 24, 1995). *Sandymount Strand* (see page 16 + 40), a book in the circular shape of that particular stretch of Irish beach on the Bay of Dublin, can be seen as another expression of Kaldewey's obsession with the language of place. James Joyce lived there and it is his descriptions of Sandymount as they appear in *Ulysses* that are at the heart of this volume. At the same time the book salutes contemporary Irish culture by including the work of two other Irishmen who have resided at Sandymount – Nobel Prize-winning poet Seamus Heaney, who contributed two new haikulike poems written especially for the book, and the artist Felim Egan who made the etchings.

Closed, Chuang Tsu's *Dream of a Butterfly* (see page 16, 42 + 89), with Chinese calligraphy and a translation by Bun Ching Lam and colored etchings by Kaldewey, himself, appears as only one half of nature's gossamer creation. Open, it plays a series of visual and linguistic games with the complex bilateral symmetry of the species. The legendary tale itself views two states of beings as mutually reflective. "One doesn't know whether it was Chung Chou dreaming that he was a butterfly, or a butterfly dreaming that he was Chuang Chou." Two overlapping double-folded triangles of Chinese paper make each page into the semblace of a wing carrying text and etching like decorative markings. And the English and Chinese versions, set in their natural order of presentation – the former beginning left, the latter right – meet at the colophon in the center.

The Gyres, a poem by W. B. Yeats (Kaldewey Edition 25, 1995) (see page 43, 90 + 91), was the text chosen by artist Richard Tuttle for his collaboration with Kaldewey. The verses set against one another two recurring "gyres," or cycles of culture. When "conduct and work grow coarse and coarse the soul," some mystery revives "the workman, noble and saint." The dominating metaphor is of something hidden and then disclosed and Tuttle invented a format in which the reader must do the same. Within the cavity created by a double-folded page, another sheet of a different kind of paper is hinged. This "vertical" page emerges for two inches below the bound sheet before it folds upward to cover the text. Sine it leave exposed the right-hand margin of the underlying sheet, that corner of the page appears lopped-off. This rather complicated pairing creates a series of variations for both reader and artist. It permits the viewer to see the image first as an independent entity and then, through his own action, joined to the text in a double-page spread. It allowed the artist to experiment with boundaries by continuing his woodcuts in different ways beyond the defining edge of one page to the contrasting surface of the other. In Tuttle's hands, the static object that is the book becomes something that shifts and changes and the first clue to its surprises is the initial view of the binding with its own disconcerting missing corner.

The title of John Ashbery's poem, *By an Earthquake* (Kaldewey Edition 23, 1993) (see page 88) refers to the grammar of destiny (as in "wounded by ... or" saved by, ...," etc.). This is the subject of the verses in which more than 45 characters (some named, others anonymous) take a hand in, or meet, their fate. The arbitrary and the disjunctive upon which we impose meaning has always been Ashbery's subject, and here it is translated visually into the multiple *500 Capp* – a Box of Fluxus style objects designed by the conceptual artist David Ireland to accompany the poem. *500 Capp* is Ireland's three-story house in San Francisco and the box is filled with materials relating to this building. Among the items are three folders with stories of the house, a piece of sheet rock, 6 "dumb balls" molded of concrete, photos of the artist's studio and, of course, the Ashbery poem, a first edition printed as Mylar posters. A type-drawer handle made at a foundry makes it easy to gain access to the elegant box created by Shahin of Albany, a family of artisans specializing in wood.

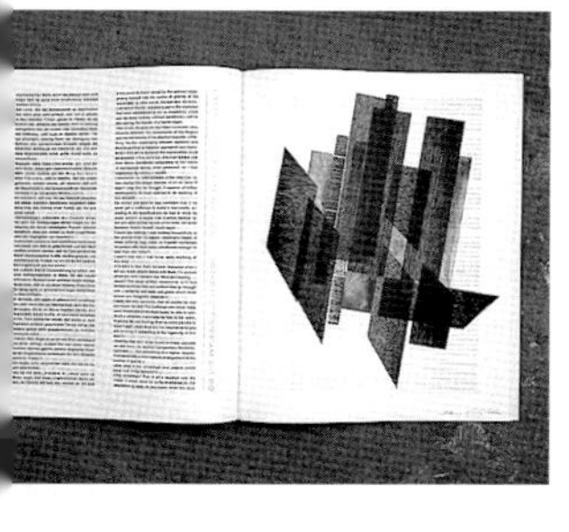

A desire to explore the expressive character of the written word can be said to characterize a third category of Kaldewey Editions. *On the Marionette Theater of Heinrich Von Kleist* by the late Arthur Cohen (Kaldewey Edition 14, 1988) (see page 17, 33, 81 + 82), is the response of a 20th-century man of letters to an article published in 1810 by Heinrich von Kleist. The book begins with Cohen's commentary on Kleist, raising provocative comments, pointing out narrative techniques, interpreting a subtext. Having Kleist's own words follow Cohen's colloquy allows the reader to join the argument across time.

The typography, design, and illustrations were done by the artist Elaine Lustig Cohen, who brought to fruition a project her husband had contemplated before his death in 1986. The two full-page abstract illustrations and six ornaments she designed were "hot printed," a technique first labeled as such by the avant-garde Dutsch printer. H. N. Werkman in the 1920's. Lustig Cohen explained her choice of this method:

... I wanted to make use of a device in the illustrations that would reflect the sensuous quality of letterpress printing so superbly realized at the Kaldewey Press. My solution was to cut out wood shapes that could be printed directly on the press... They would then be used both to illustrate and ornament the text.

Sand aus dem Urnen (Kaldewey Edition 22, 1994) (see page 41 + 87), the second selection of poems from Paul Celan's *Mohn und Gedächtnis* conceived by Mischa Kuball, appeared after a hiatus of ten years instead of the intended five. It was a far more ambitious volume containing twenty poems with fifteen original black acrylic drawings made by the artist for each of the sixtyfive copies in the edition. Continuing to explore the theme of absence he had so successfully evoked through the paper cut-outs in the first volume, Kuball now turned to the words themselves to suggest this motif. The peom appear in two versions side by side on the page – the one for the eye is set in type; the second, for the hand, is done in braille. Presented in these two forms on the thick grey paper used for the blind, the words, paradoxically, seem to gain in density as they disappear from sight. This combination of weight and evanescence occurs once again in the deluxe edition where the metal sheets from which the braille is printed are embedded in the cover of the book and painted by Kuball with the image of an hour glass (see page 87). They evoke the conclusion of Corona, one of the most beautiful poems in this volume.

Es ist Zeit das der Stein sich zu blühen bequemt,
das der Unrast ein Herz schlägt.
Es ist Zeit das es Zeit wird.
Es ist Zeit.

Writings as a demonstration of obsession, the obsession of the scribe, the author, and his fictional alter-ego, motivated Hans Peter Willberg to do a calligraphic version of Kafka's *Der Prozess* (*The Trial*, Kaldewey Edition 18, 1990) (see page 37). His manuscript, printed on silkscreen by Atelier Limited, Münster, transfers to 60 pages the 250 pages of the first edition of Kafka's masterpiece. Starting with a page of 33 lines. Willberg added a line a day and as space got short, began to use a smaller and smaller hand until he was forced into illegibility by writing the lines over each others. As the last few pages become an impenetrable scrawl, their analogy to K.'s never-ending bureaucratic entanglement is clear.

The fascination of the letter forms in which canonical texts were first written is at the heart of the Kaldewey Editions of the Hebrew *Song of Songs* (No. 16, 1990) and the Latin *Metamorphosibus Appolinis et Daphnes* by Ovid (No. 19, 1992). But, true to the credo of the press, a contemporary note is struck in each of these, by way of illustration, additional text, or conceptual devices.

Kaldewey, himself, created the yellow, green, and purple paper pulp images for the *Song of Songs* (see page 35, 84 + 85). With their indistinct contours, these semi-abstract forms which allude to the religious and sensual themes of the verses, seem to float behind the solemn march of the Hebrew letters. Kaldewey, having no knowledge of Hebrew was forced to rely on his memory when setting the letterforms for the book. Since this made it necessary to send the finished pages to a proofreader, it amuses him that the one book he printed without being able to read it, is nearly the only one published without a typo.

A year in Rome and a visit to Herculaneum inspired Kaldewey to print the tale of Apollo and Daphne from Ovid's Metamorphosis in the lapidary Latin majuscules of the monuments he saw there. The edition (see page 38 + 86) is presented in three separately bound volumes, which fit like a puzzle in a tray case. The first holds Ovid's version in Latin, the second a modern variation in English by the American poet Mary Caponegro who tells the tale from Daphne's point of view, and the third houses the colophon. Colored images by Kaldewey are scattered through the texts suggesting fragments of ancient ruins.

In *The Wind,* a poem by the young Tibetan writer Lha Gyal Tsering (Edition Kaldewey, 26, 1996), Tibetan calligraphy with its steady, unbroken, march of contiguous letterforms creates a sober facade in front of playful wood-block tondons of the seven lucky personal gems. Secular poetry is contemporary poetry in Tibetan culture, having been written only since 1959 when the monks were forced to give up their exclusive control of education. By focusing on the wind through four seasons, Lha Gyal Tsering, expresses the constant sense of movement and change of his native Amdo in Northeast Tibet, a landscape populated by nomads. Transformation is always before the reader's eyes in these verses as the wind races through the abandoned summer camps of the nomads in winter or releases the manacles of clear cold water in spring or writes its name across a lake in the summer heat. Each season's symbolic color – the blue of winter, green of spring, yellow of summer, red of fall – precedes its stanza via a single colored sheet and is then integrated into the poem by the colored inking of the tondos and borders. The colors appear once more as paper strips trimming the edge of the pages of the English version. Both the translation and the calligraphy were done by Pema Bhum, a member of the cultural Ministry of the Dalai Lama in Exile, and Visiting Professor of Tibetan Literature in Bloomington, Indiana.

The Wind (see page 26 + 92) follows the traditional Tibetan book form in consisting of loose sheets printed only on one side. The paper covers of the regular edition, however, although made of the very strong Daphne fibers of Tibet, are a variation on local custom. In Tibet, papers made of these fibers are dried for days in special baskets. At Kaldewey's request, the Tibetan papermaker allowed the pulp left over in the baskets to dry further and the thick, hard sheets that emerged, marked by the distinctive woven texture of their containers, are a perfect introduction to the mood of the pages within. The ten copies of the deluxe edition have covers of magnolia wood especially carved by Migmargyalpo Lama in Kathmandu (see page 26).

Bun Ching Lam is given ample room in what Kaldewey calls a "giraffe folio" for the elegant Chinese calligraphy with which she transcribed *The Great Learning* from Confucius (Kaldewey Edition 16, 1990 – 91) (see page 36). The artist Not Vital then embellished each page with a pencil line running down the middle and occasionally encircling a word. This was his conceptual stand – in for of the Western reader who glances through the text but understands nothing except the physical beauty of some of the letters. For those Westernes who wish to penetrate further, there is a translation by Ezra Pound at the close of the volume, which delights with surprising turns of phrase. "The Great Learning," it begins [is] "grinding the corn in the head's mortar to fit it for use," and continues "it is rooted in watching with affection the way people grow."

Making free with Confucius, one could say that the Kaldewey Press has been, is, and will continue to be an enterprise in which one man "watches with affection the way people grow." In a time when many cultural enterprises ape the size and ambition of the multi-national corportation, the Kaldewey Press in the person of Gunnar Kaldewey, testifies to the power of an individual's vision energetically pusued. Over the ten years of its existence, so far (and there is more to come), the Kaldewey Press has published (and Kaldewey has printed) thirty-nine limited-edition books in twelve languages with a large international group of contemporary artists. Through these volumes, Kaldewey has single-handedly built a community that gives artists, writers (of the present and the past), binders and other artisans the chance to speak in their tongues to us all.

List of illustrations

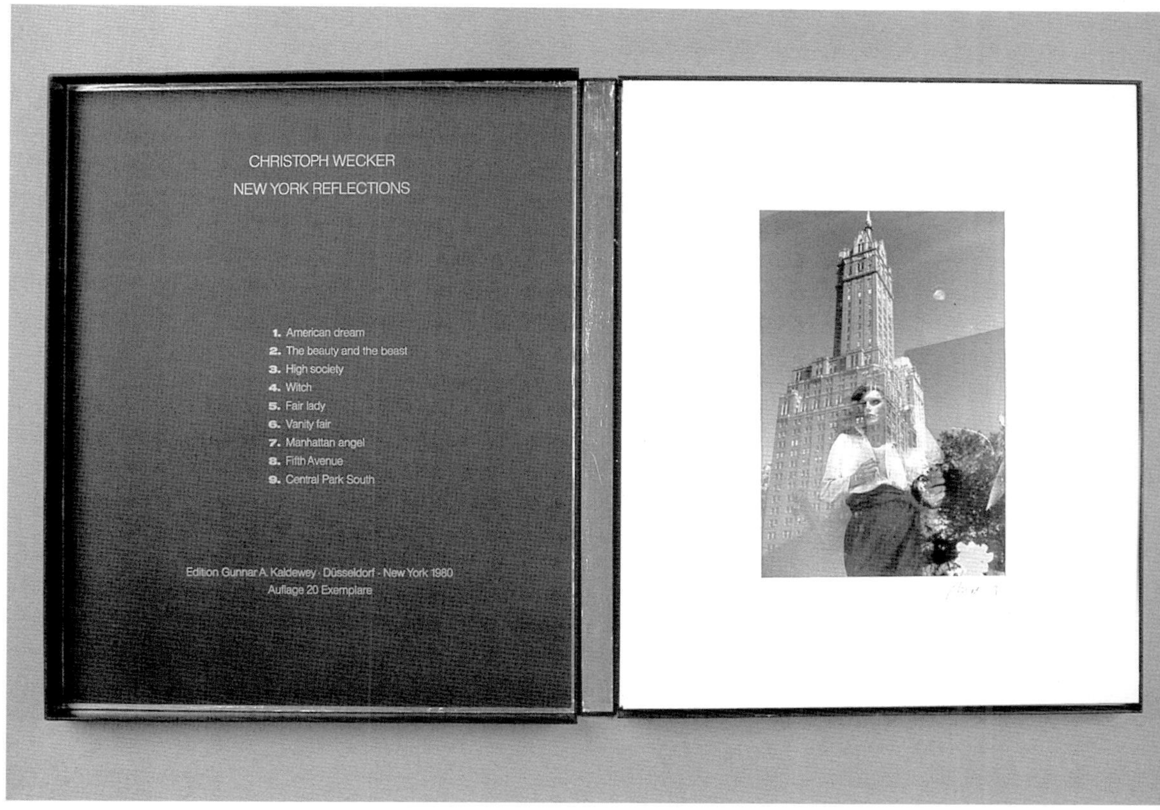

1

New York Reflections.

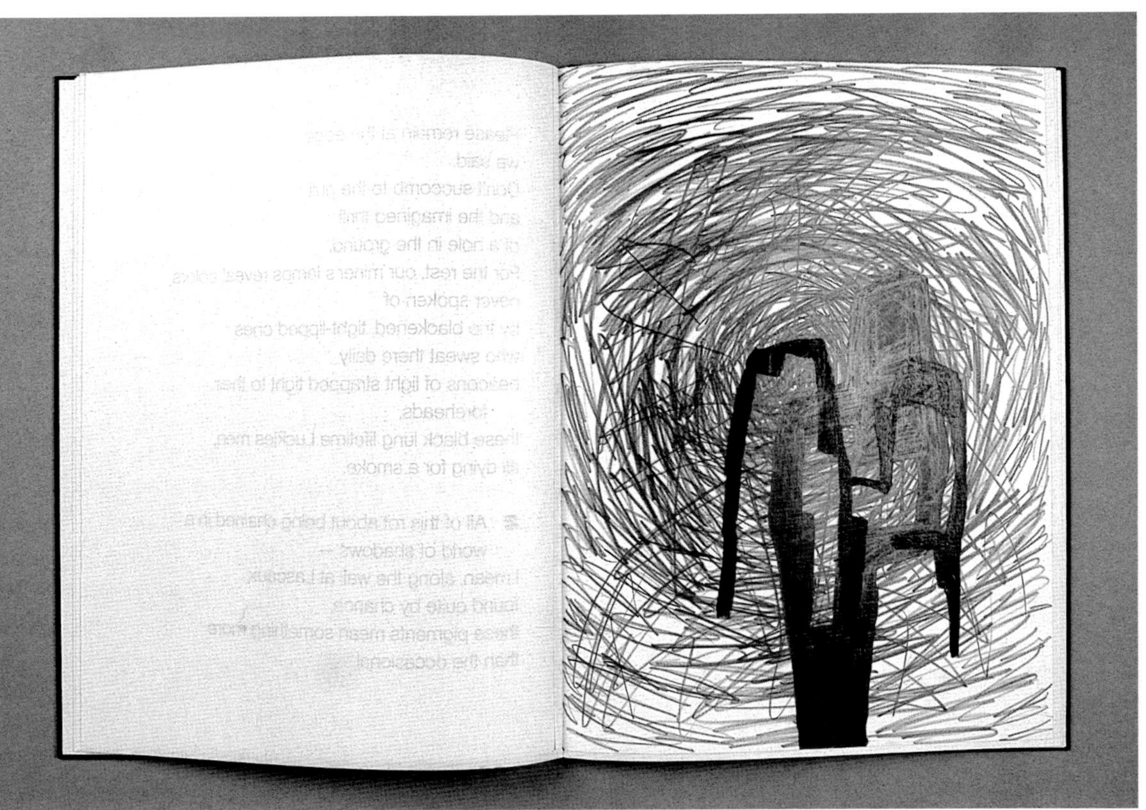

2

Everett Potter, Cave Pictures.

Original drawing by Jonathan
Lasker.

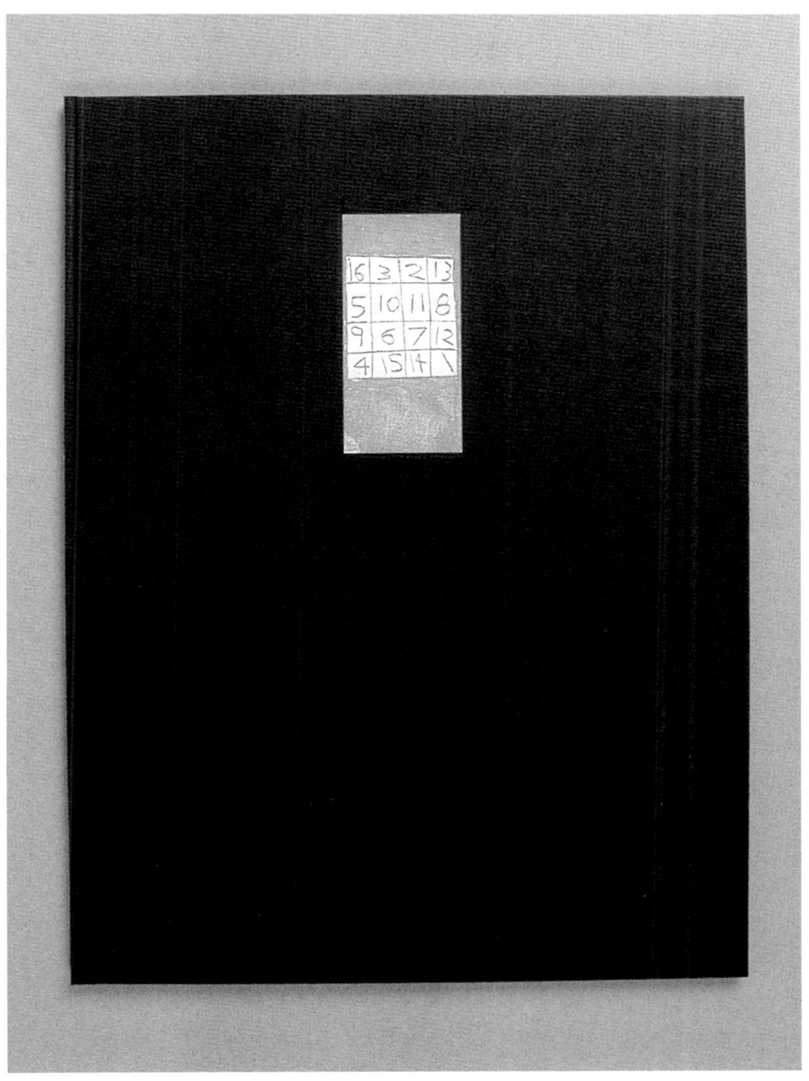

5

**Sample of the binding style
of early Edition Kaldewey
books.**
Bound by Christian Zwang.

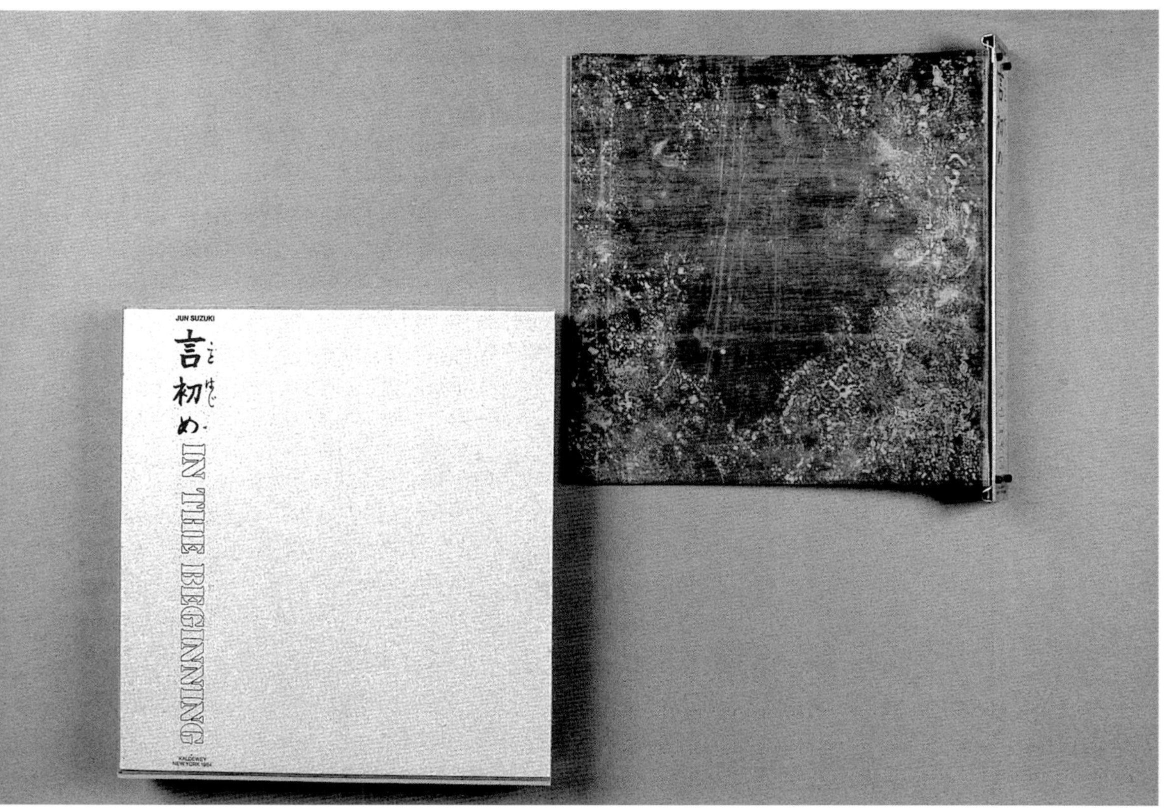

7

In the beginning.
Box and metal book.

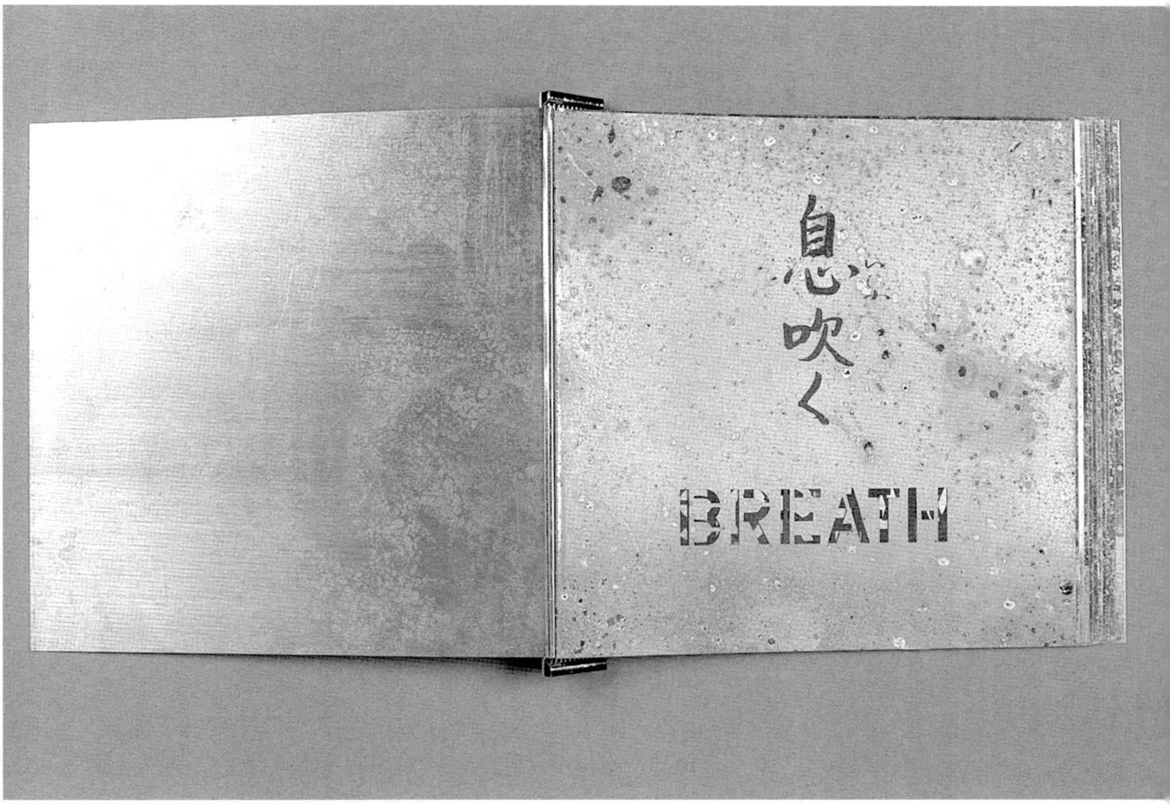

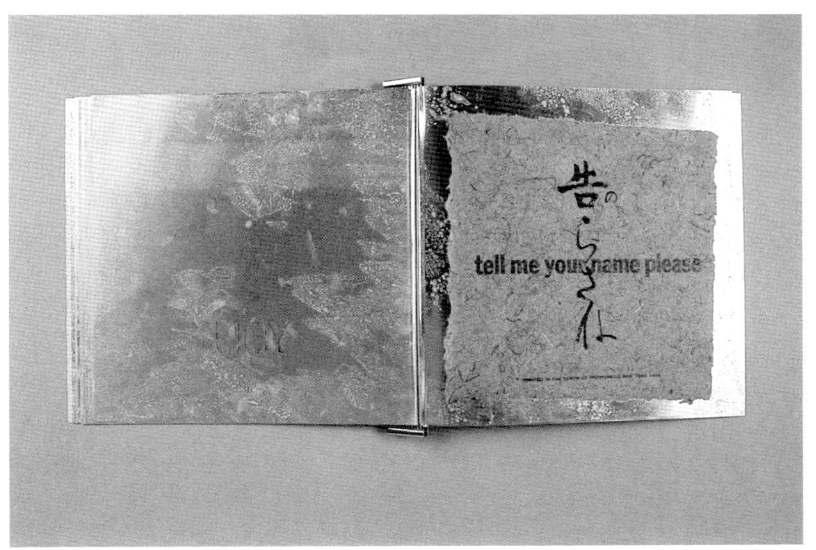

In the beginning.

Metal book of Jun Suzuki.

Colophon of the metal book.

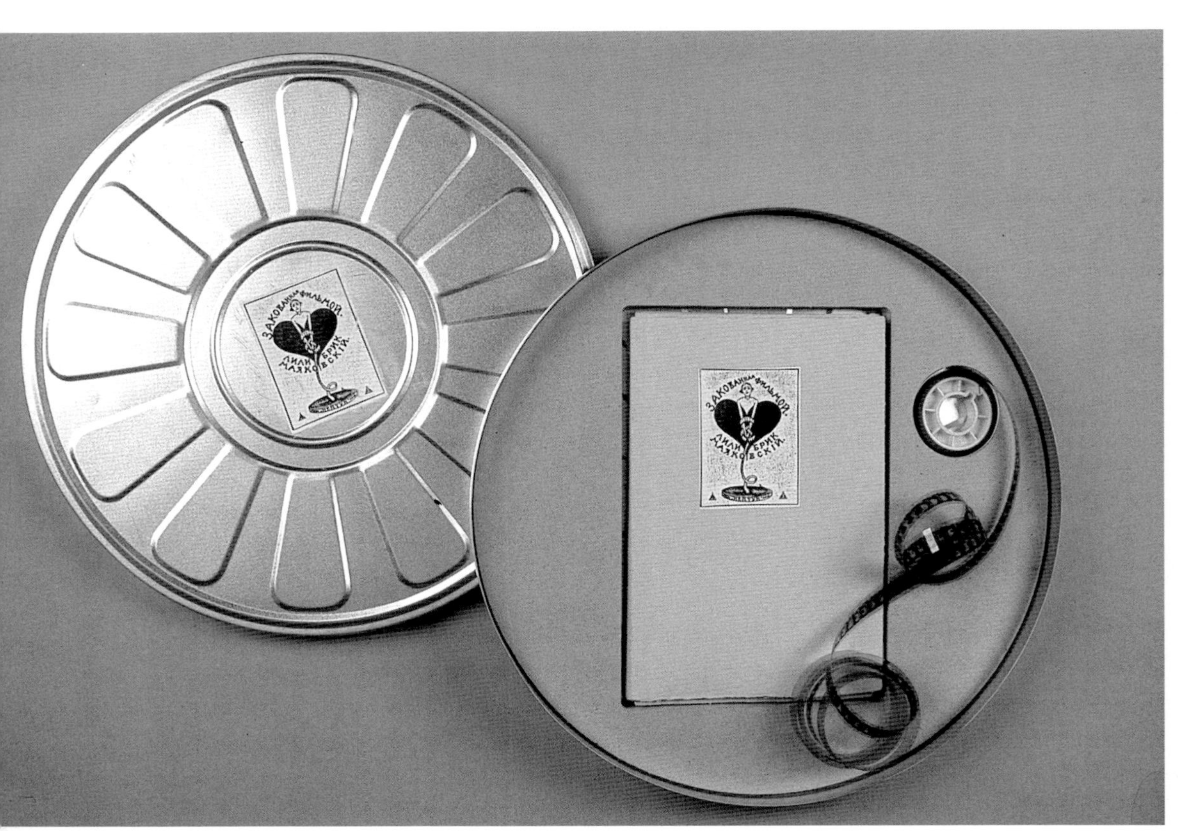

8

Wladimir Mayakowsky,
The celluloid heart.
Film can.

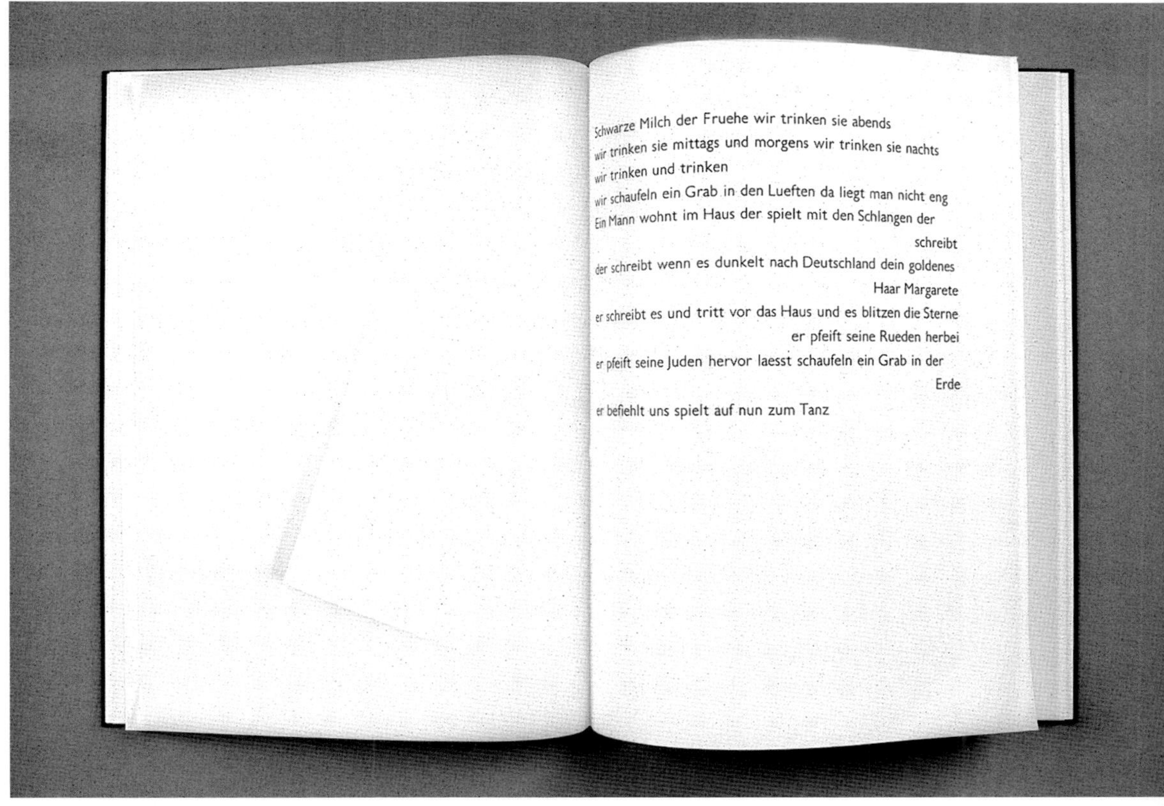

9

Paul Celan, Todesfuge.
Paper cuts by Mischa Kuball.

27

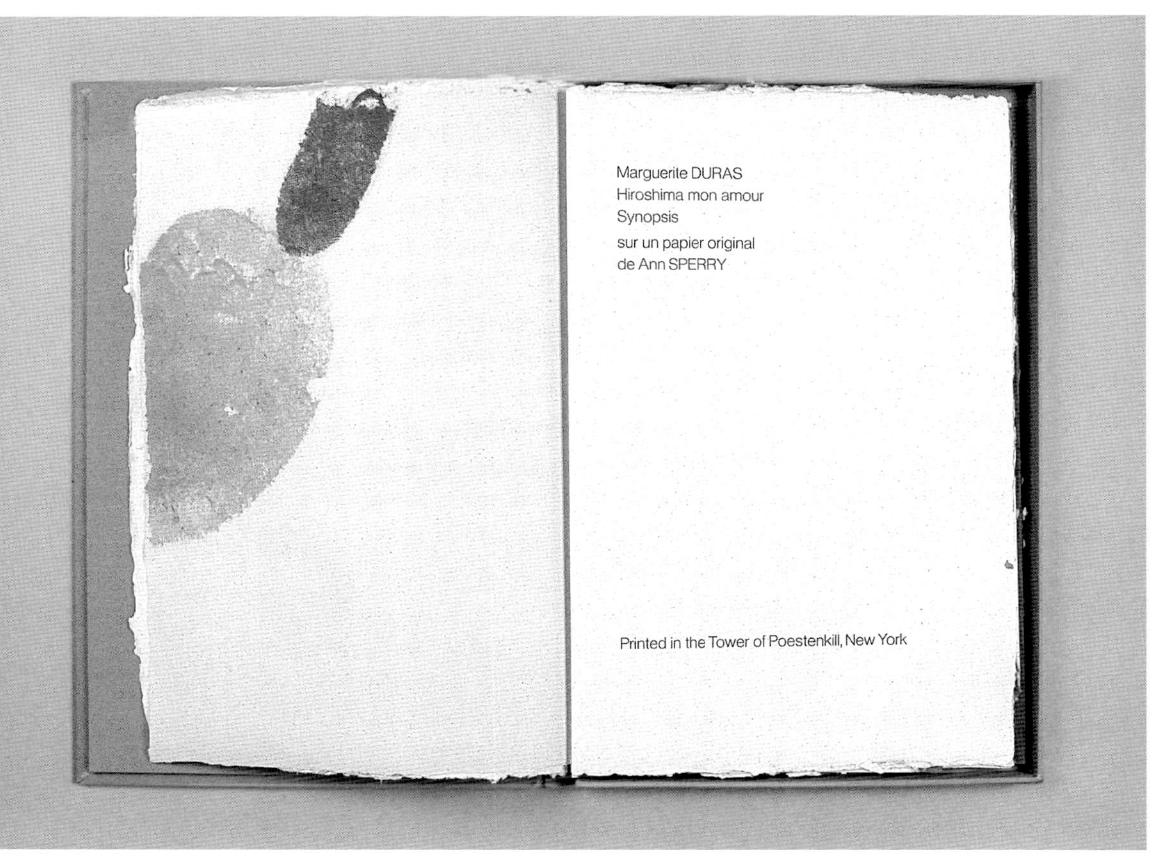

10

Marguerite Duras,
Hiroshima Mon Amour.
Paper pulp images by
Ann Sperry.

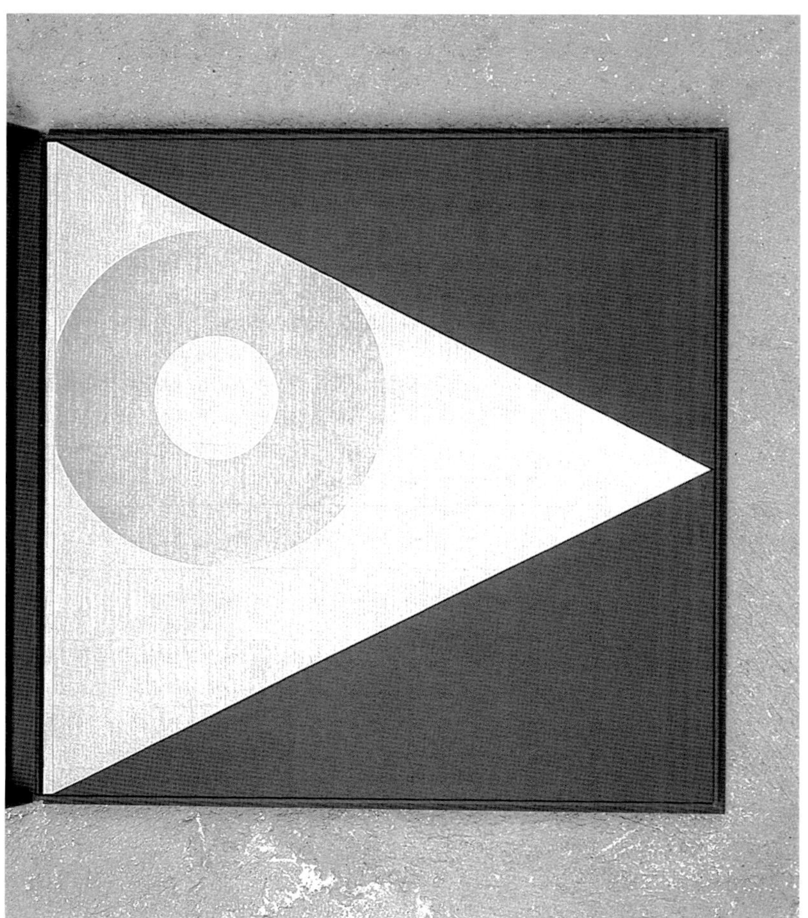

11

Samuel Beckett,
Quatre poèmes.
Triangular shape book with
etchings and one record by
Chinese composer Bun-Ching
Lam.

Box by Christian Zwang.

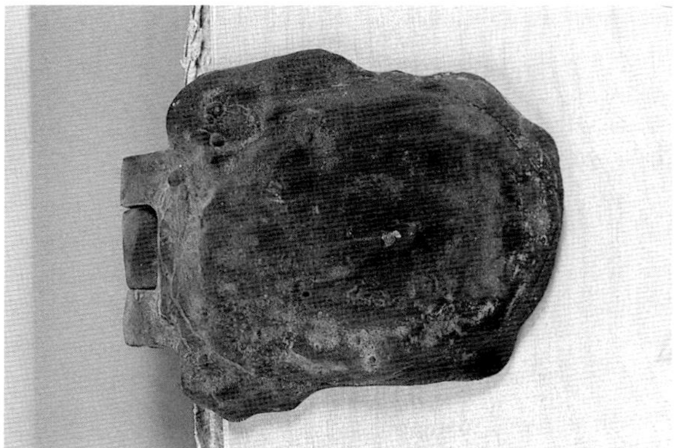

12

Not Vital,
Poesias rumantschas.
Binding of Russian birch with
bronze hinges by Not Vital.

Bronze hinges,
cast in Pietro Santa, Italy.

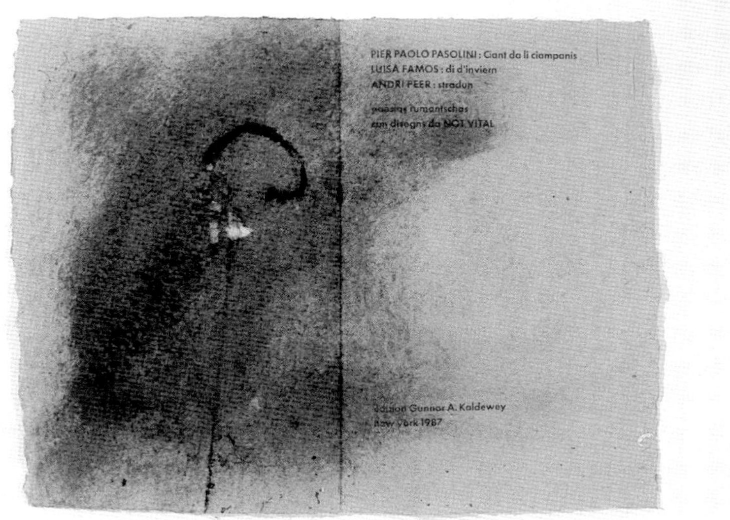

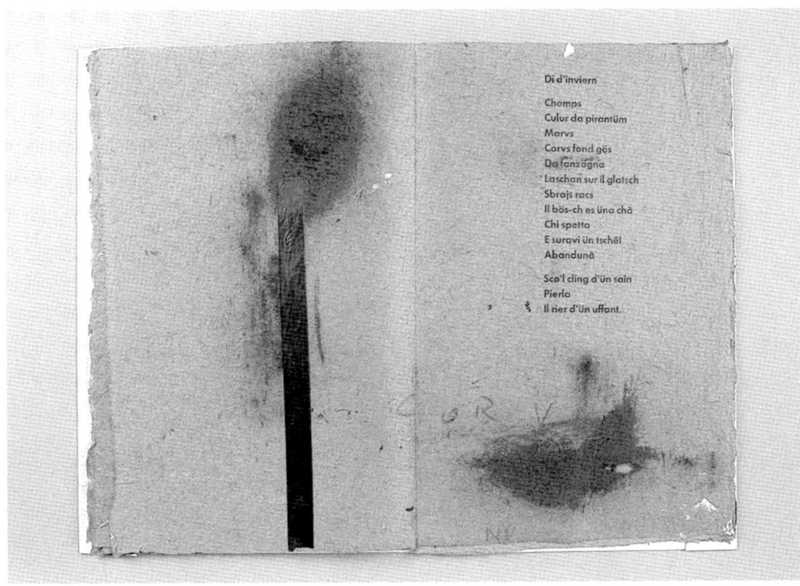

Not Vital,

Poesias rumantschas.

Cover and wooden box.

Title page.

Luisa Famos, Stradun.

Original drawing by Not Vital.

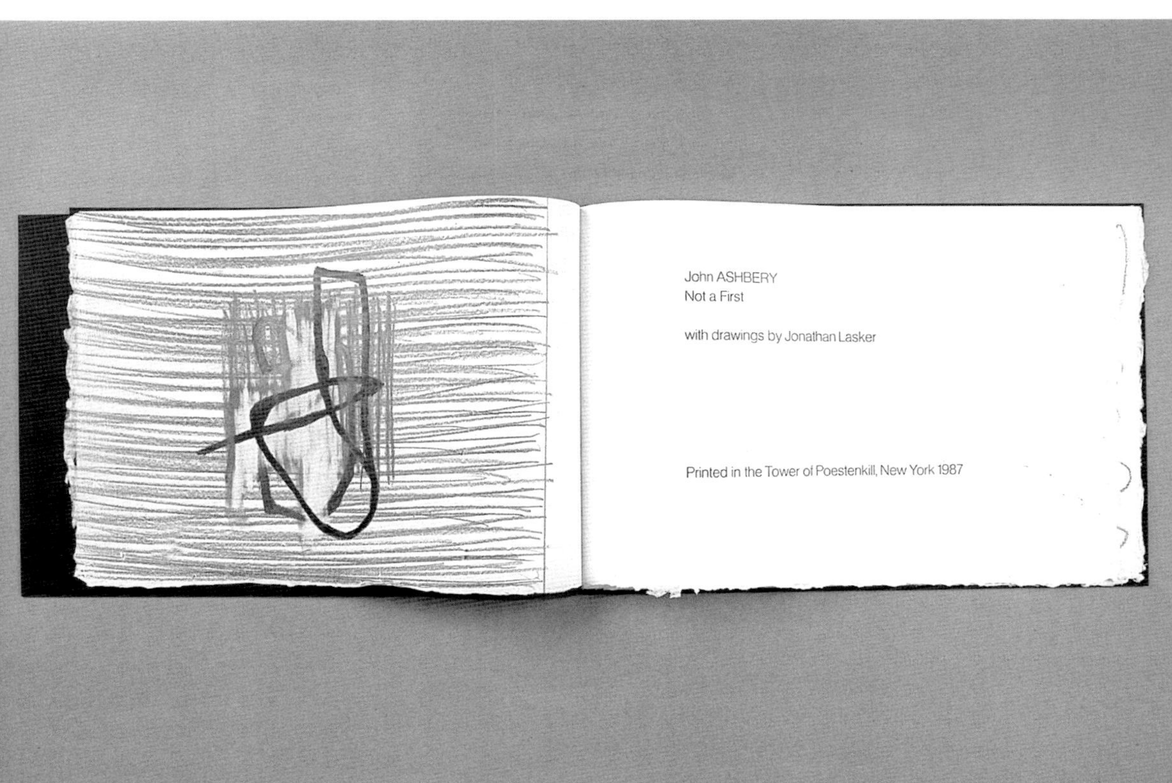

13

John Ashbery, Not a First.

Original drawings by
Jonathan Lasker.

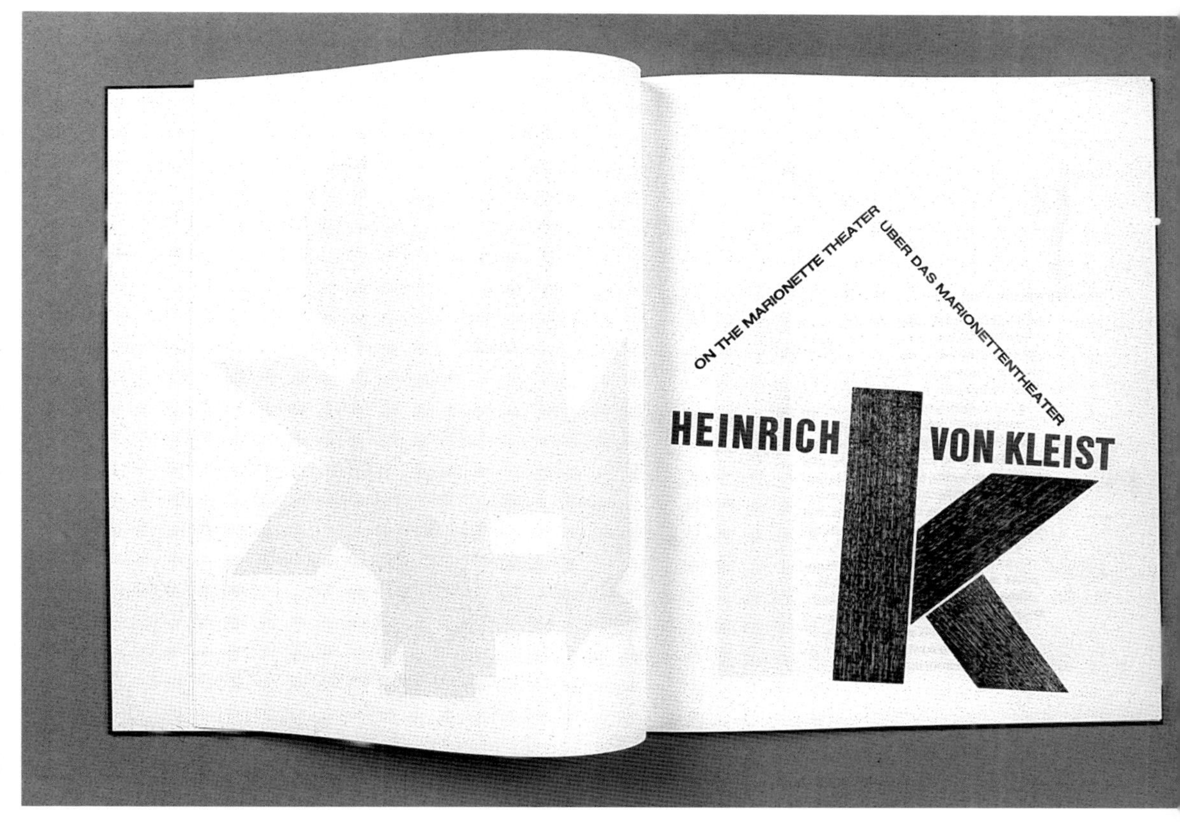

14

Arthur Cohen,
On the Marionette Theater
of Heinrich von Kleist.
Title page designed by
Elaine Lustig Cohen.

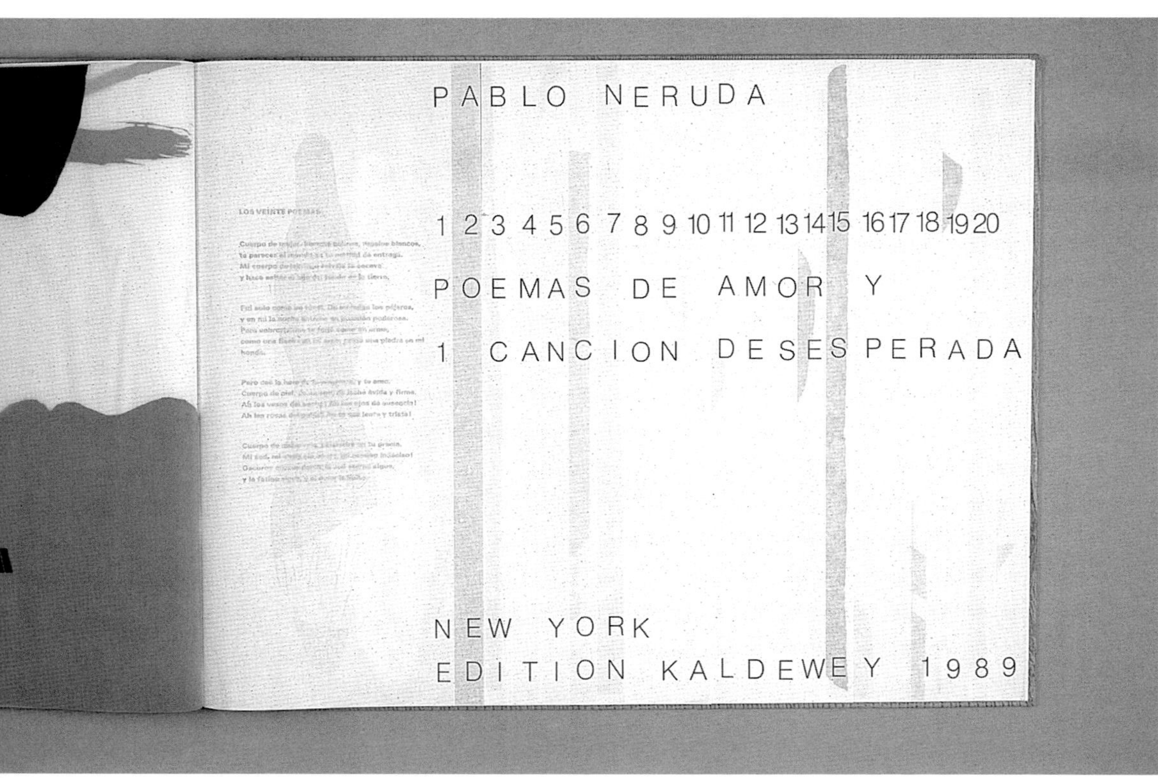

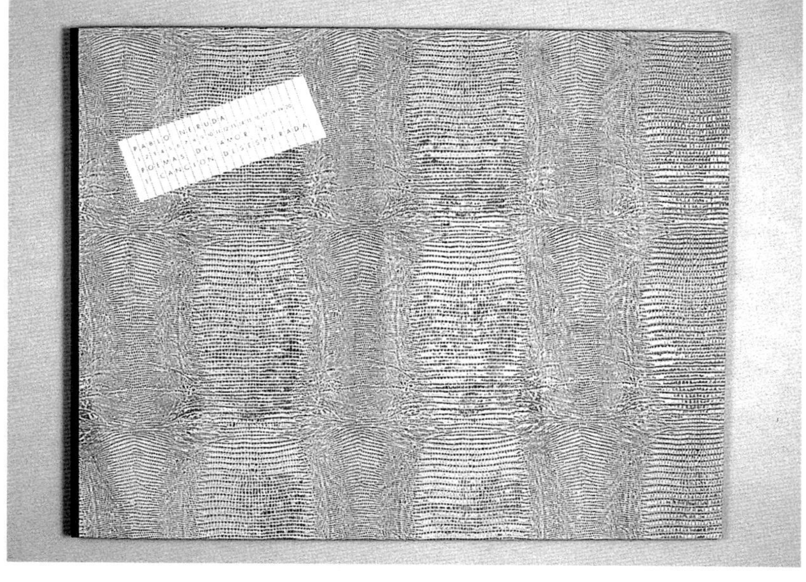

15

Pablo Neruda,
20 poemas de amour.
Title page for the deluxe
edition on Chinese paper.

Leather binding by
Christian Zwang.

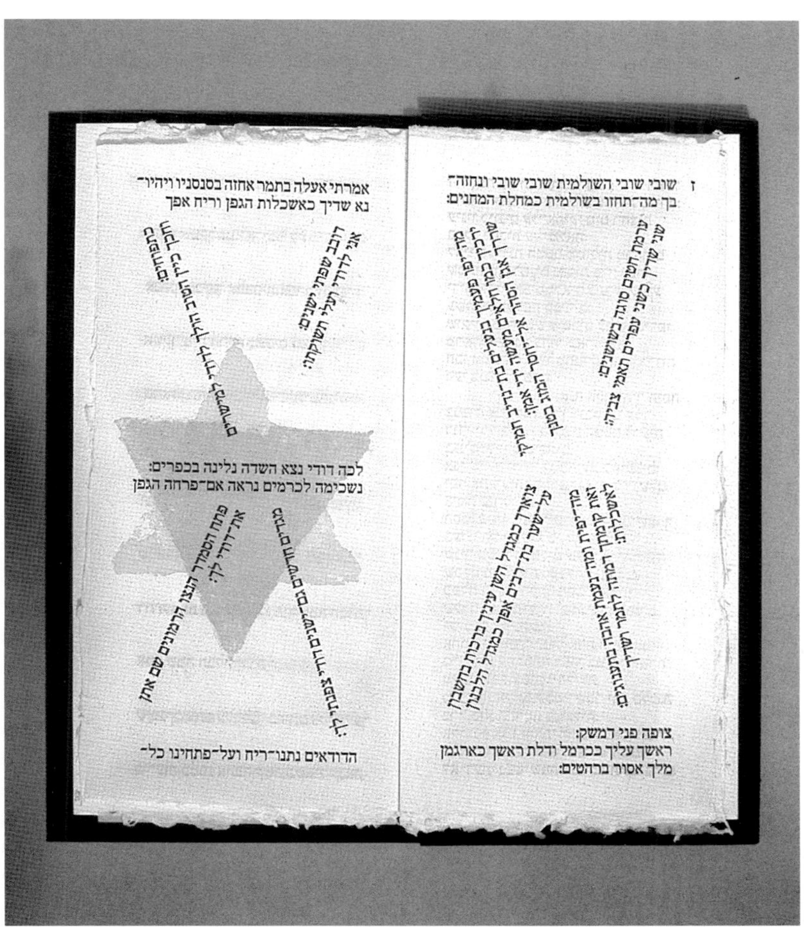

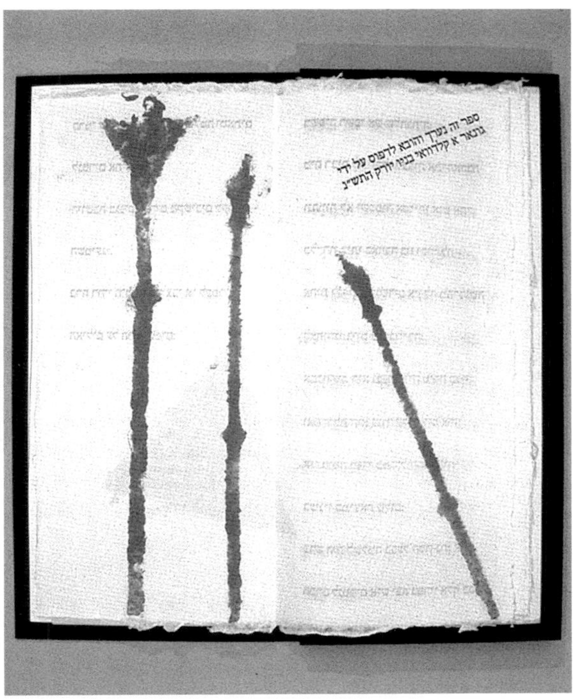

16

Šir Haširim le Šelomo,
Song of Songs.

Colophon page.

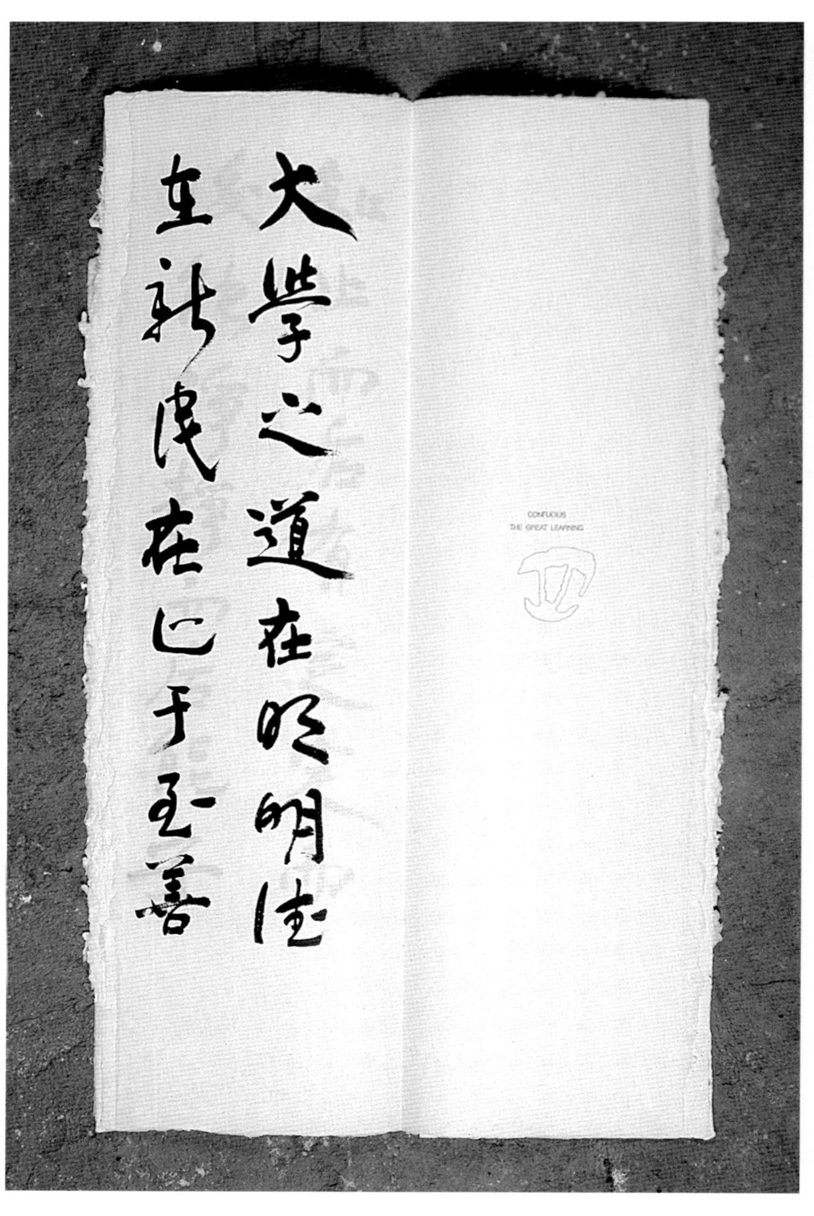

17

Confucius, The great Learning.
Title page. With calligraphy
by Bun-Ching Lam and a translation by Ezra Pound.
Drawings by Not Vital.

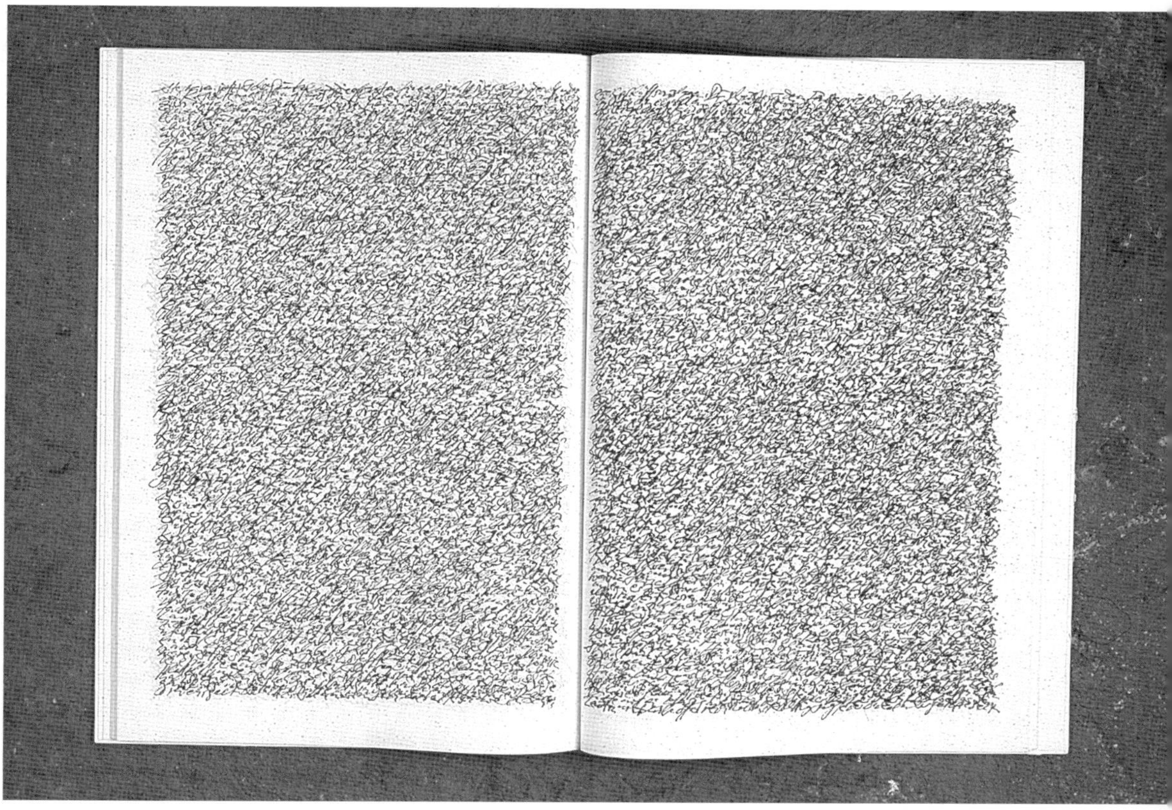

18

Franz Kafka, Der Prozess.
Calligraphy by Hans Peter
Willberg.

Flexible paper binding by
Christian Zwang.

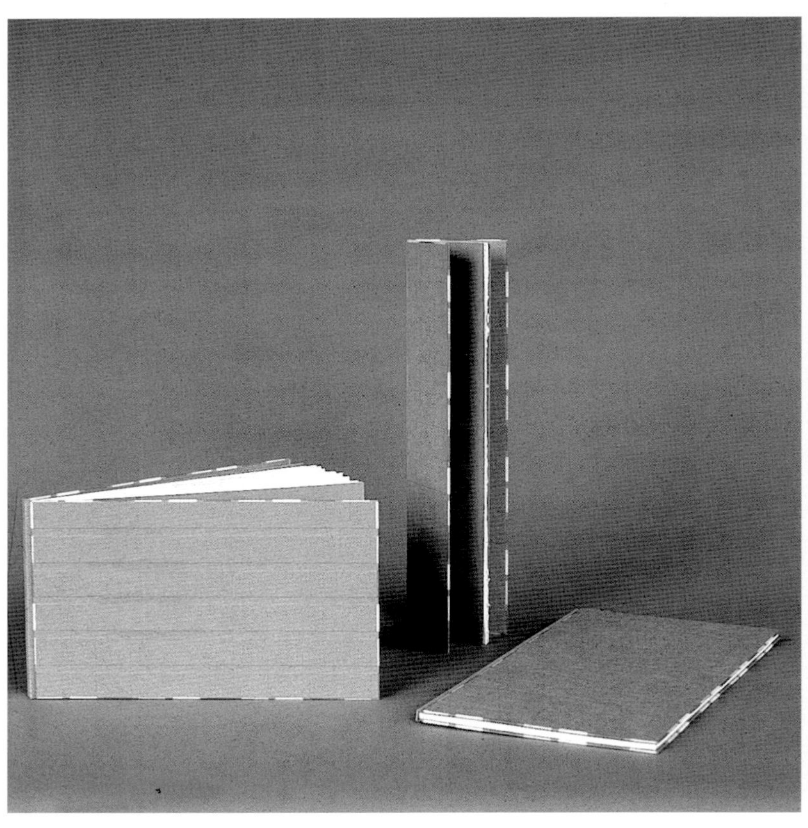

19

Ovid, Metamorphosis.
A book in three parts.

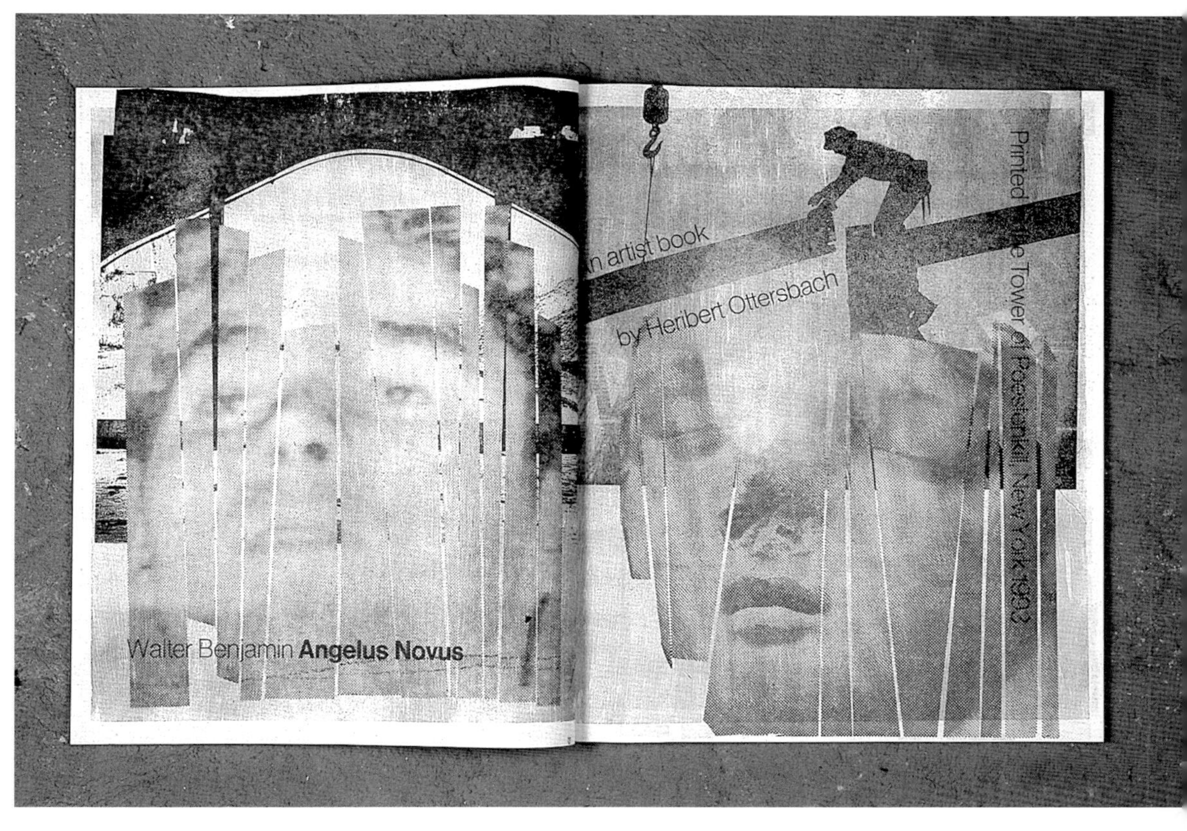

20

Walter Benjamin,
Angelus Novus.
Title with woodcuts by
Heribert Ottersbach.

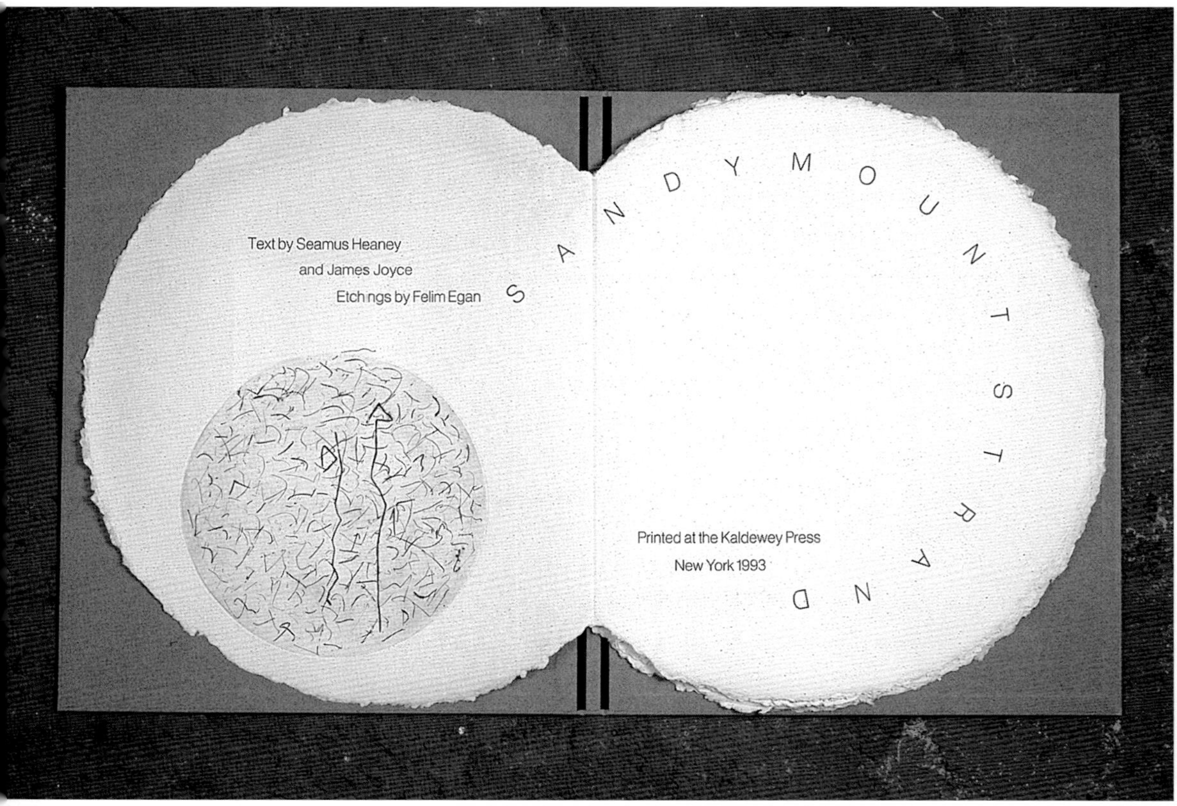

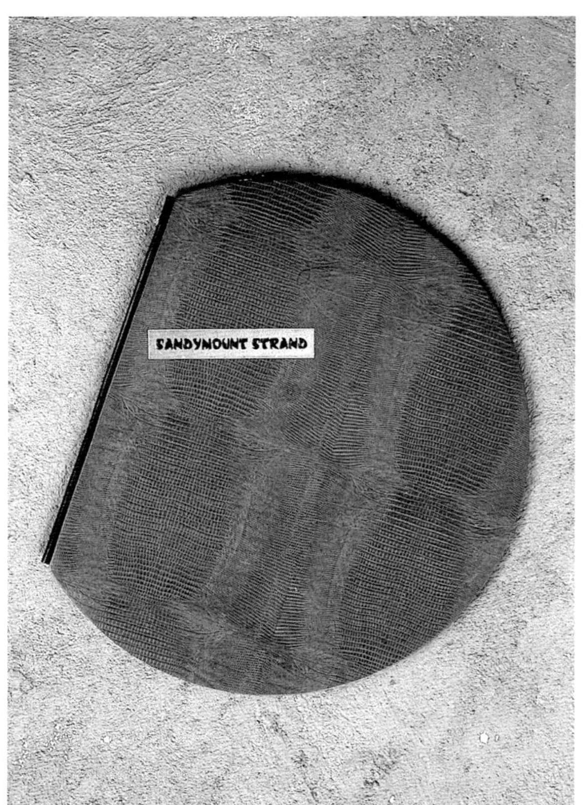

21

Sandymount Strand.

Text by Seamus Heaney and
James Joyce.
Etchings by Felim Egan.

22

Paul Celan,
Sand aus den Urnen.
Original drawing by
Mischa Kuball.

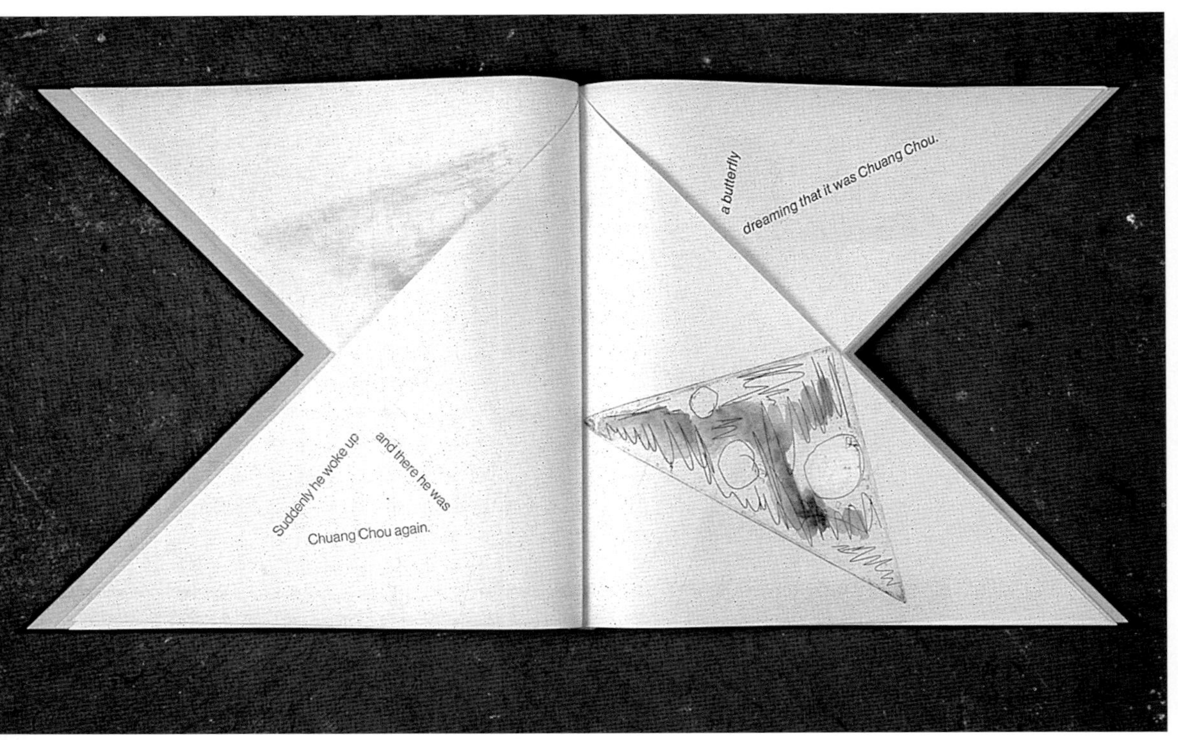

24

Chuang Tsu,
Dream of a Butterfly.
English and Chinese text.

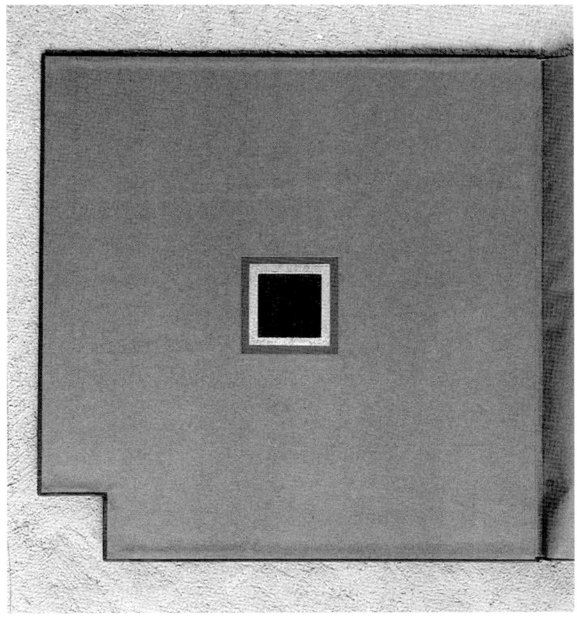

25

The Gyres.
(Source of Imagery.)

Leather binding.
Doubloure by Richard Tuttle
for the deluxe edition.

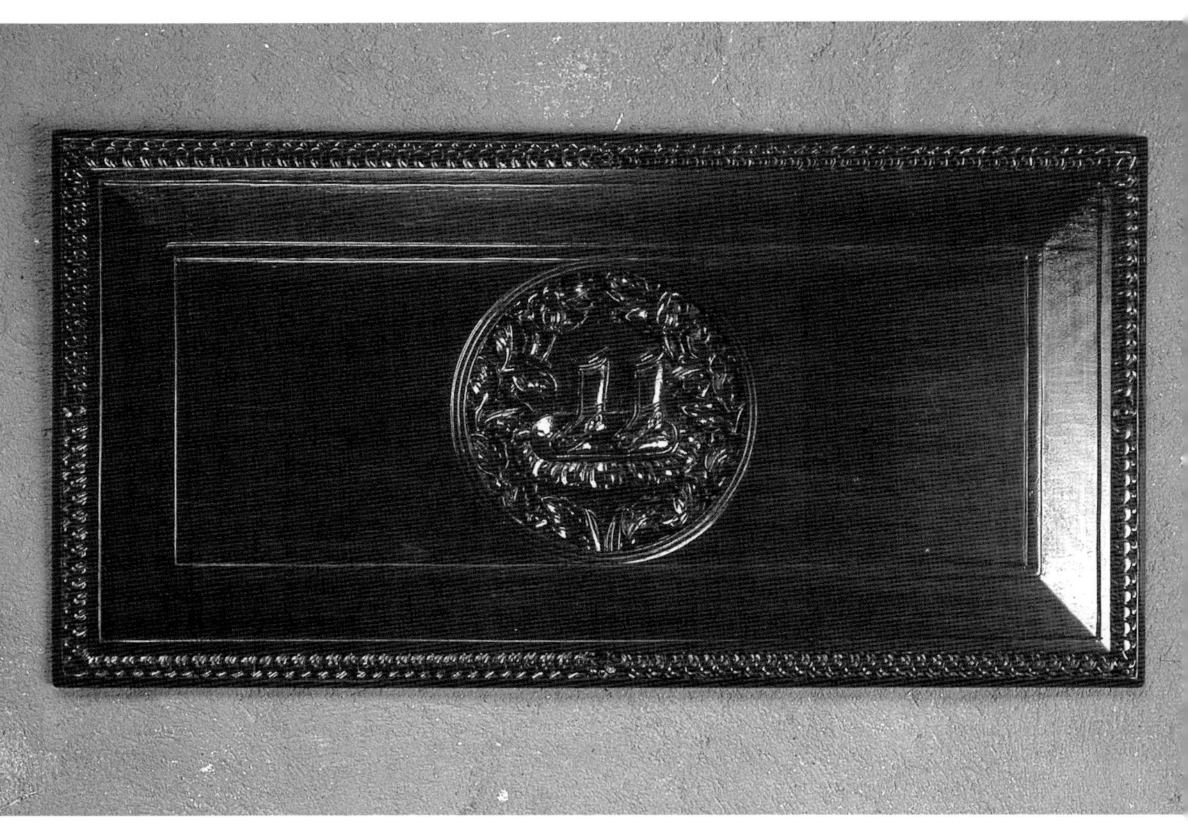

26

Lha Gyal Tsering,
The Wind.
Wooden cover for the deluxe
edition of the Tibetan book.

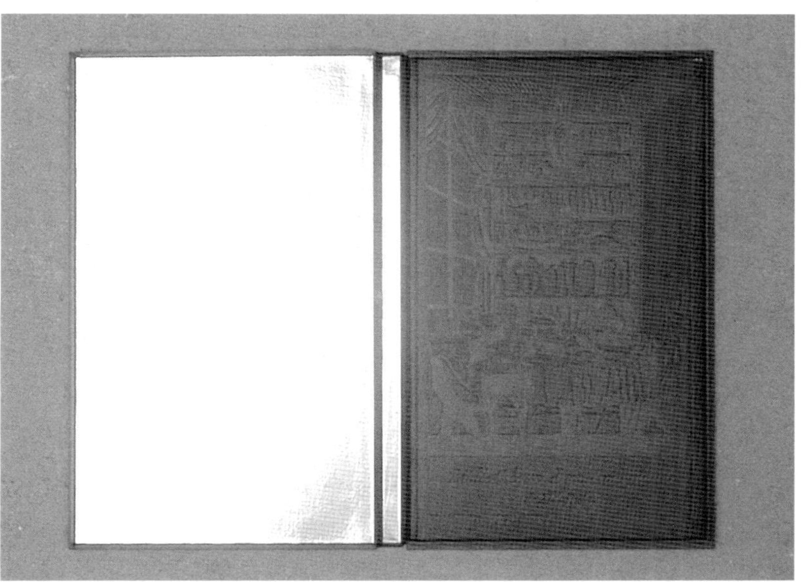

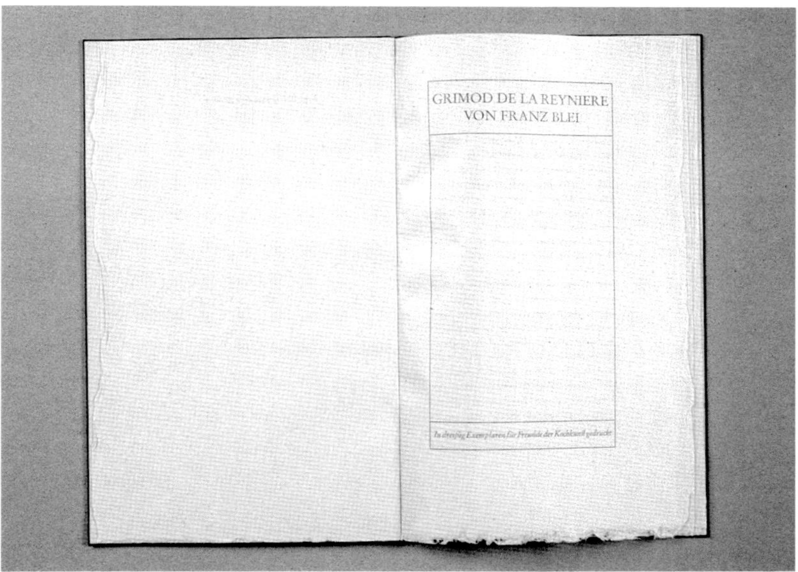

0

Grimod de la Renière.
First book by Gunnar A. Kaldewey, made for fellow members
of an all-male cooking club.

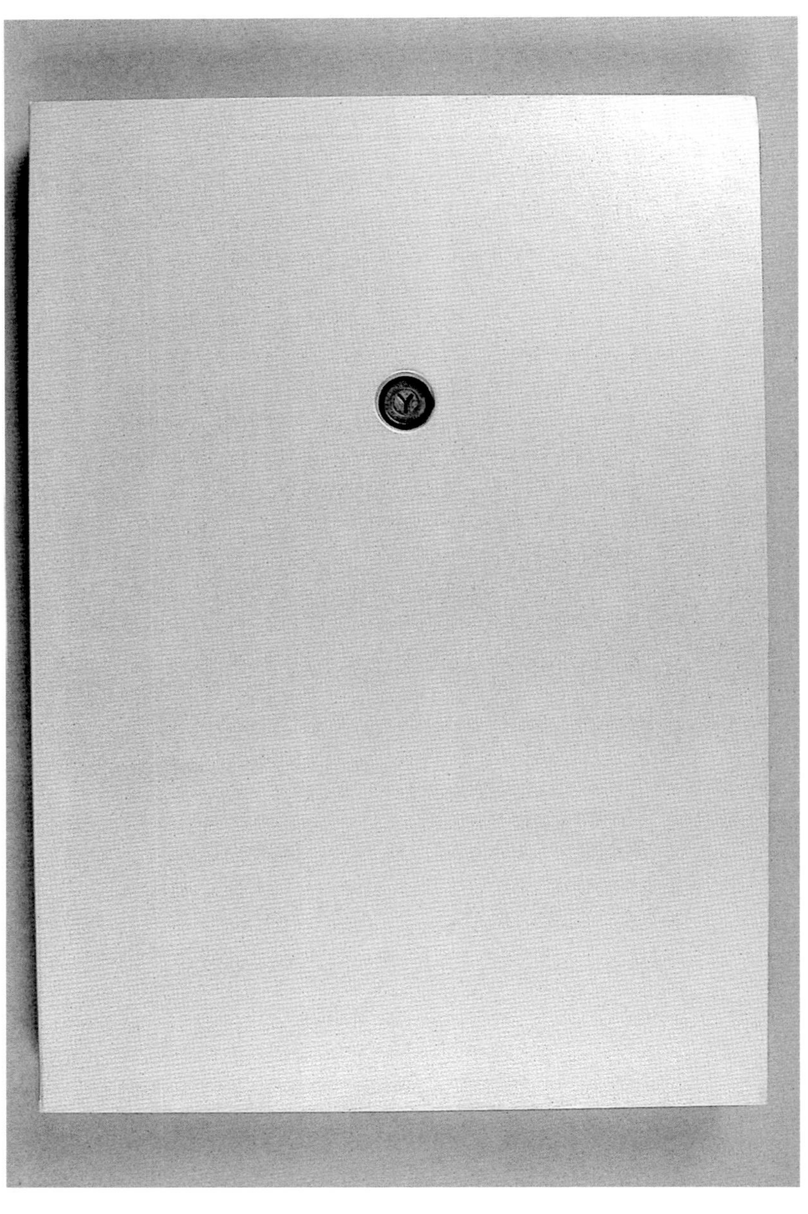

1

New York 1977.

Silver box with subway token.

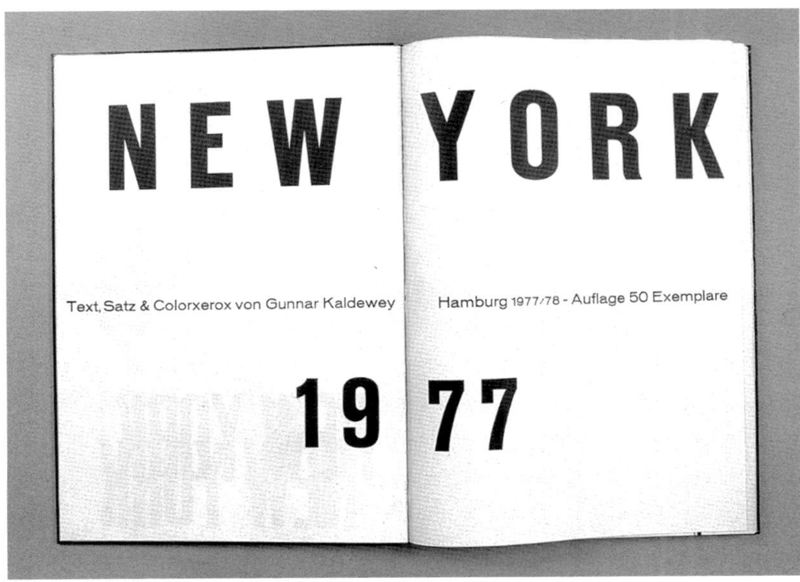

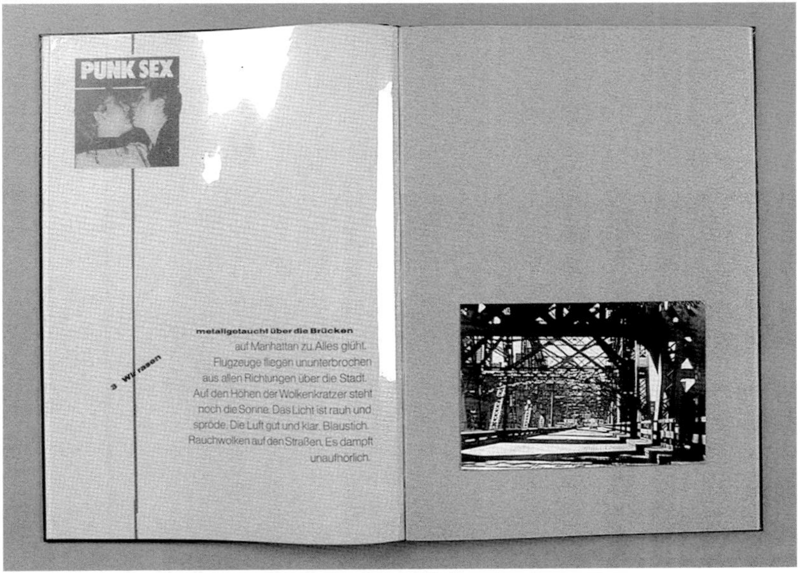

New York 1977.
Pages of aluminum and
sand paper.

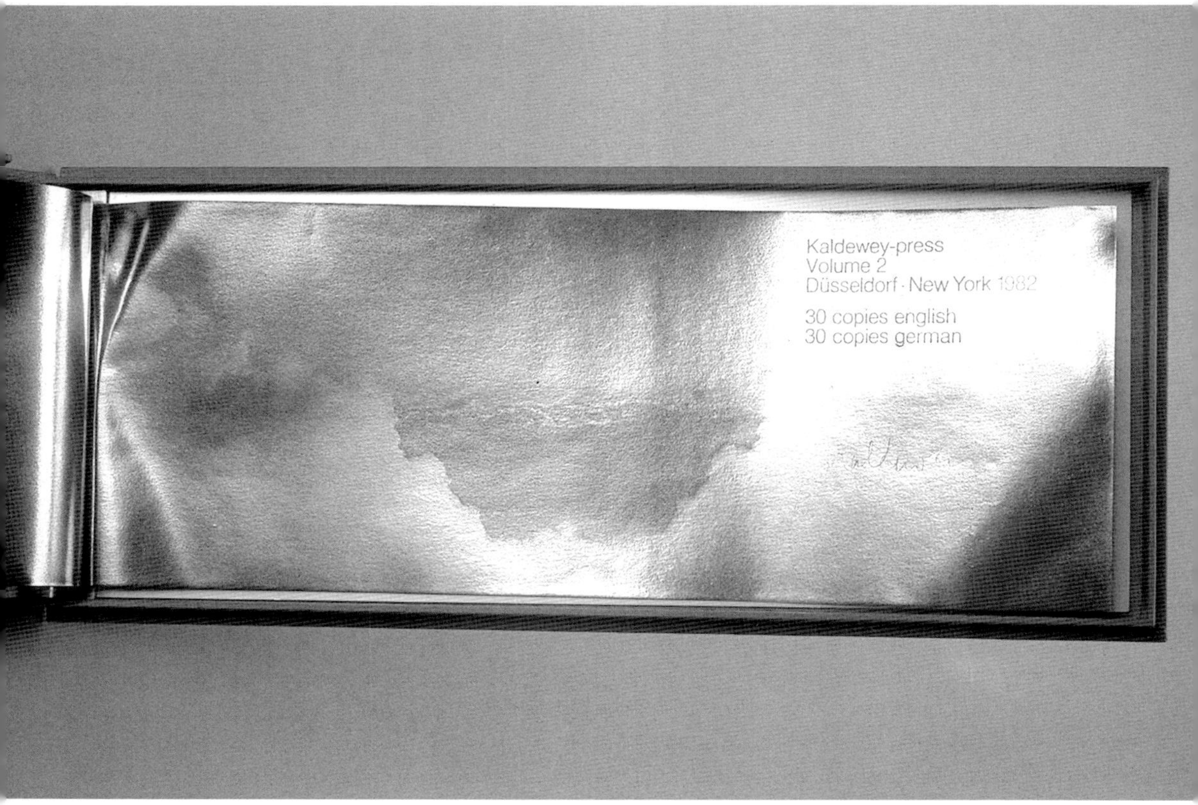

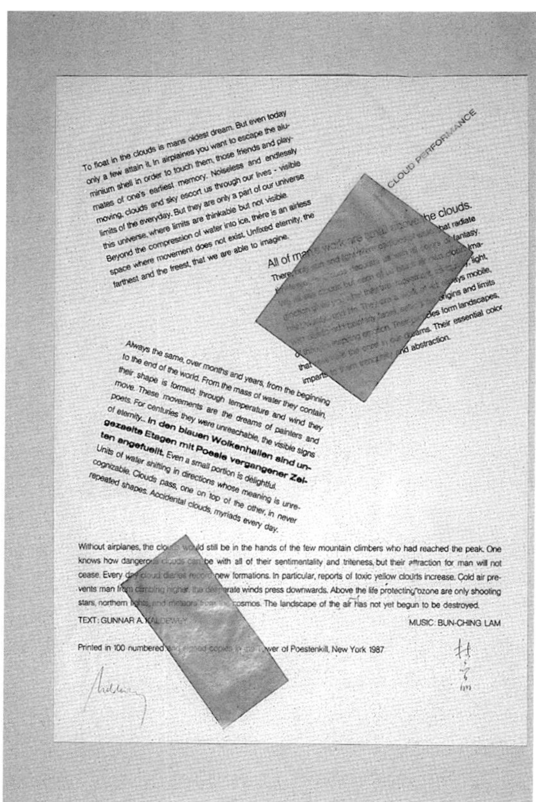

2

Clouds · Wolken.

Aluminum pages.

Poster for Clouds.

Dropped from a helicopter for

a music performance in Seattle.

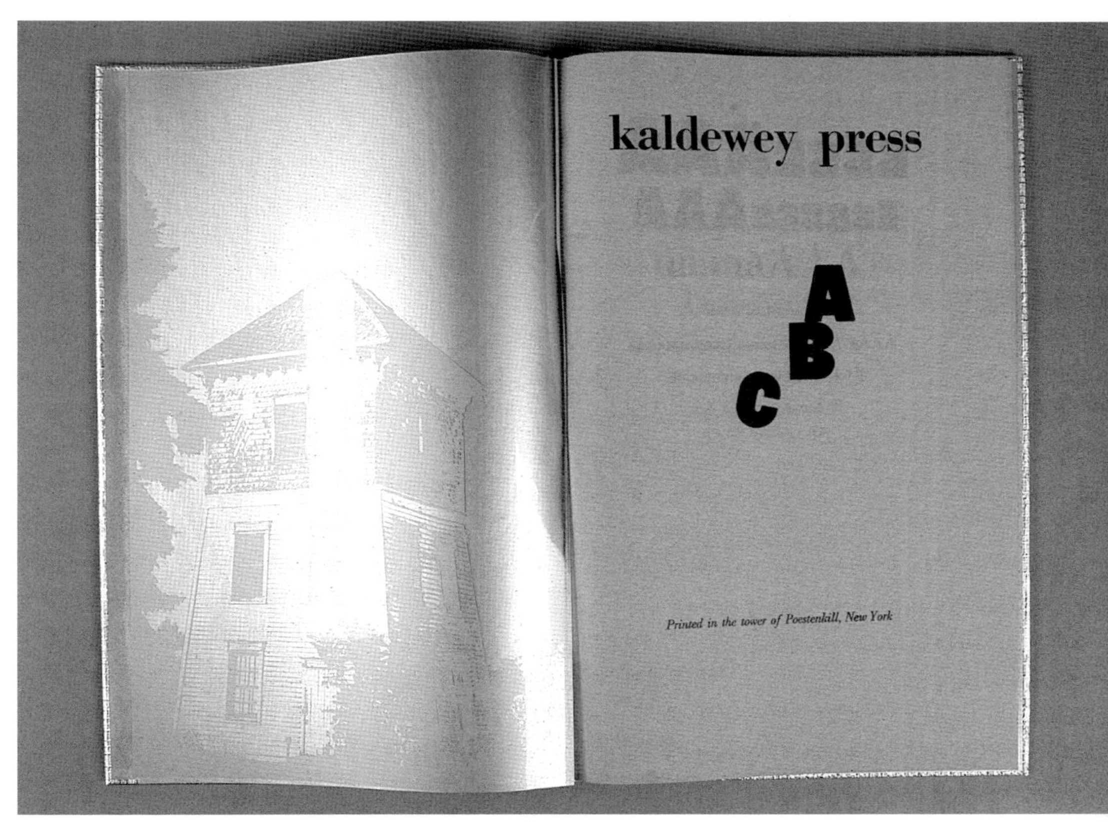

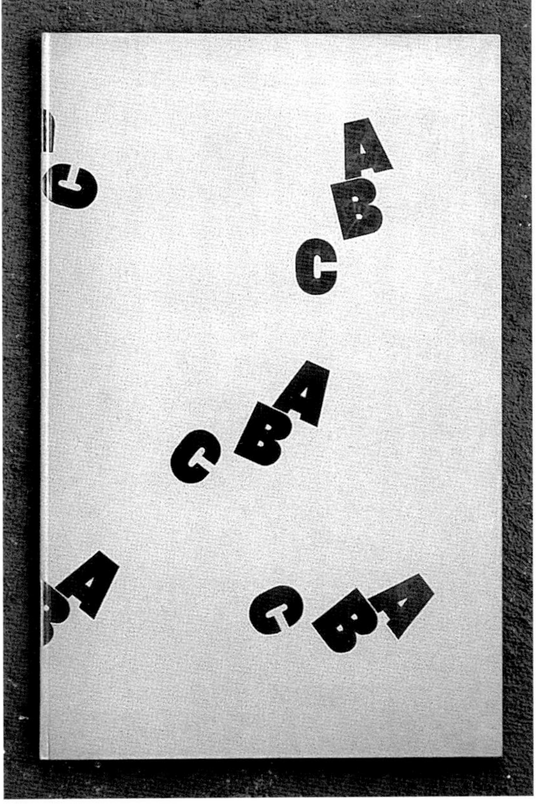

3

ABC Book.

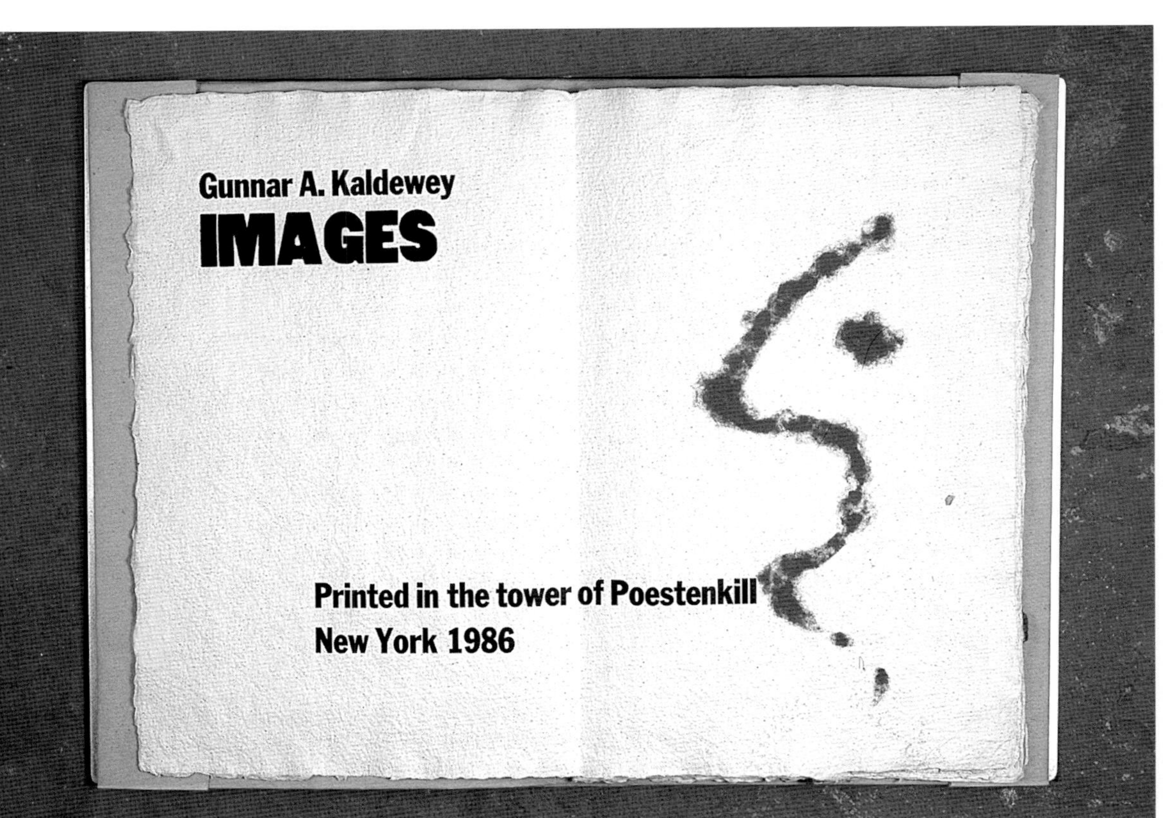

4

Images.

Title page.

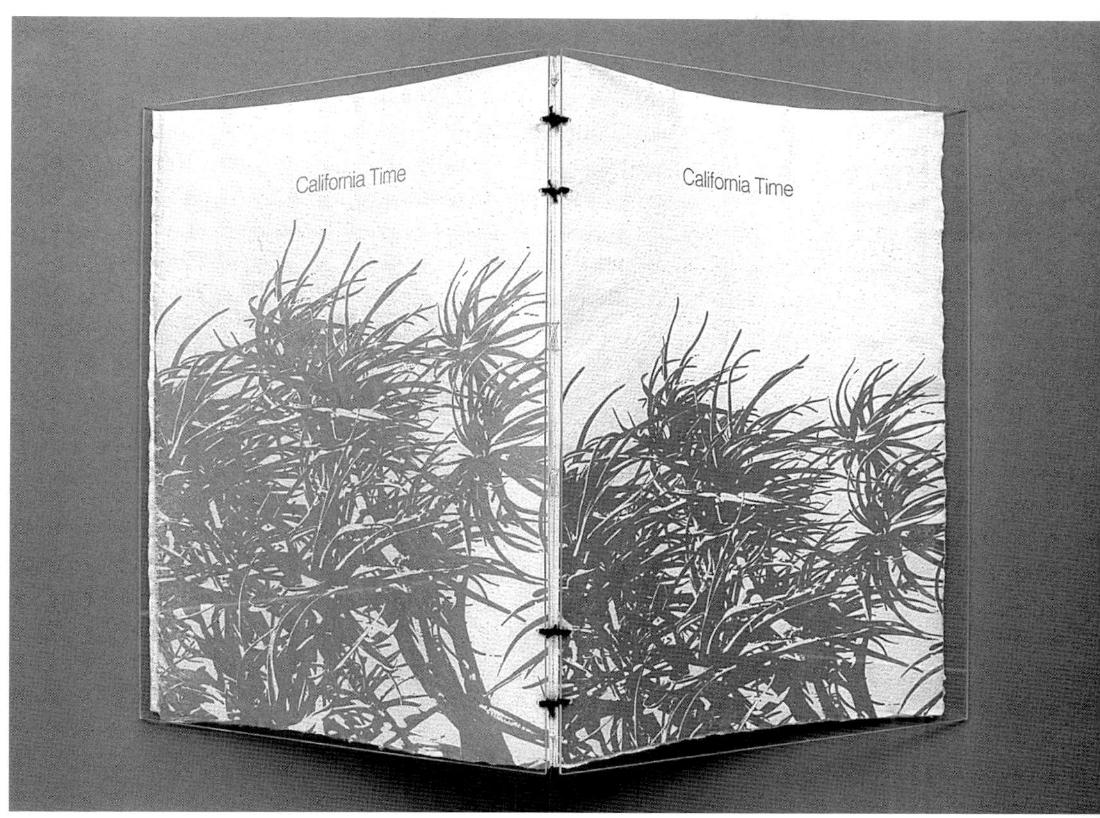

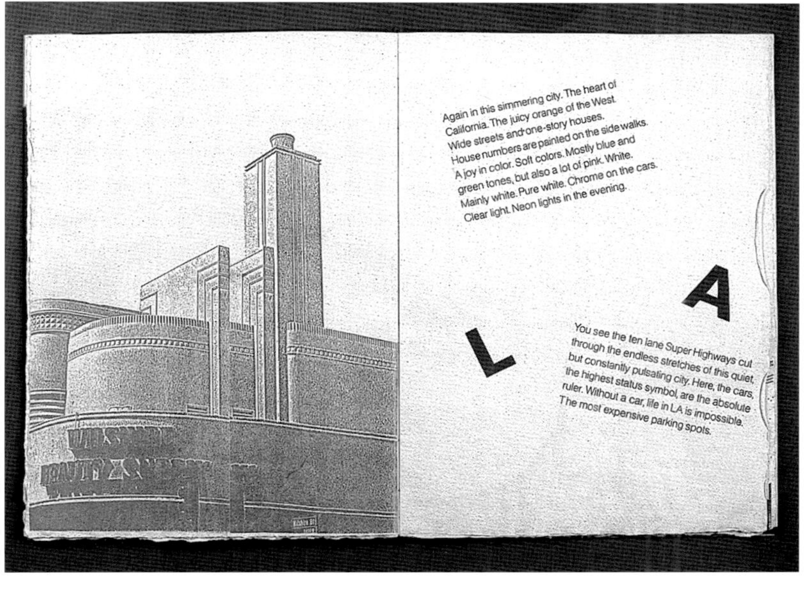

5

California Time.

Plexiglas binding.

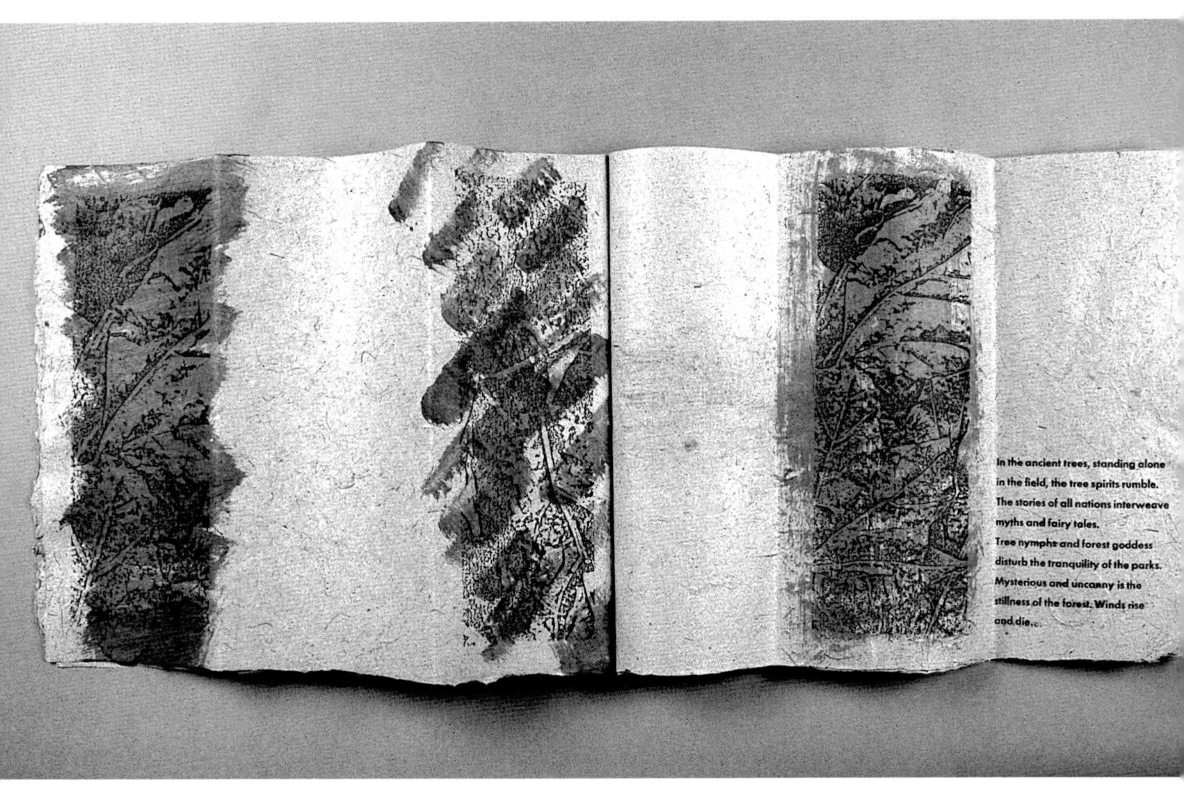

6

Trees.

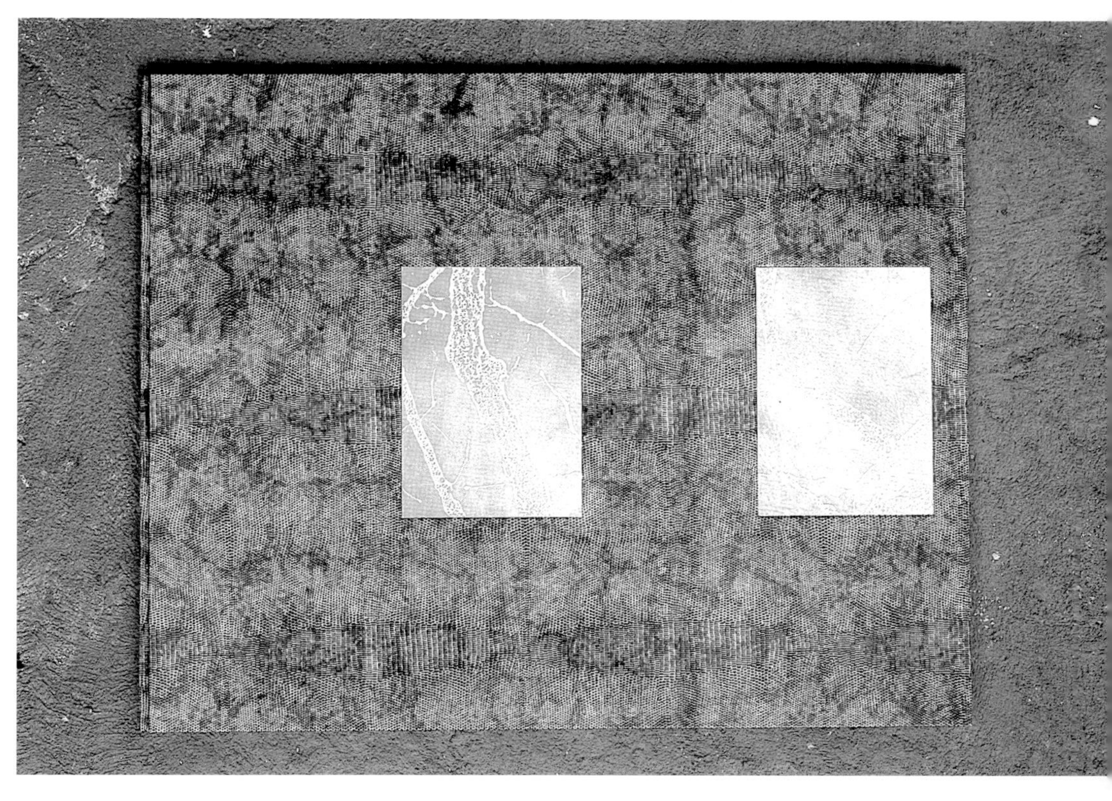

Trees.
Deluxe edition with Dutch
Chagrin paper.

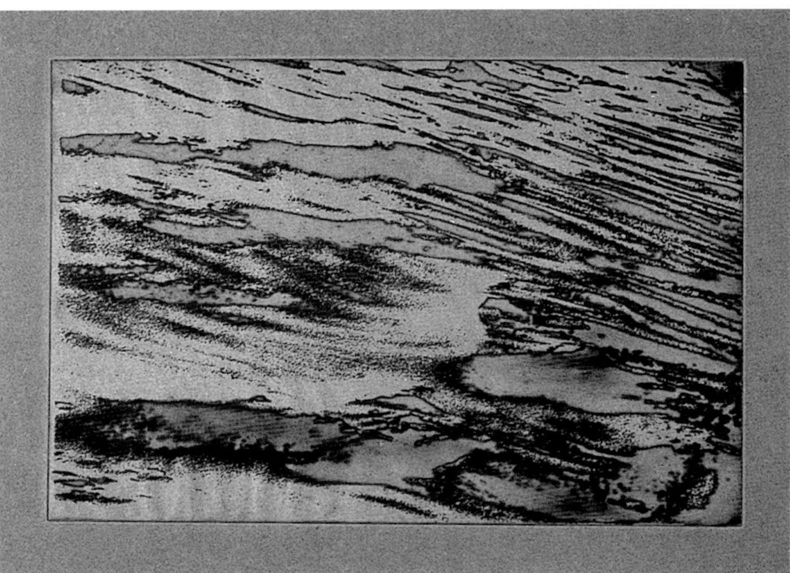

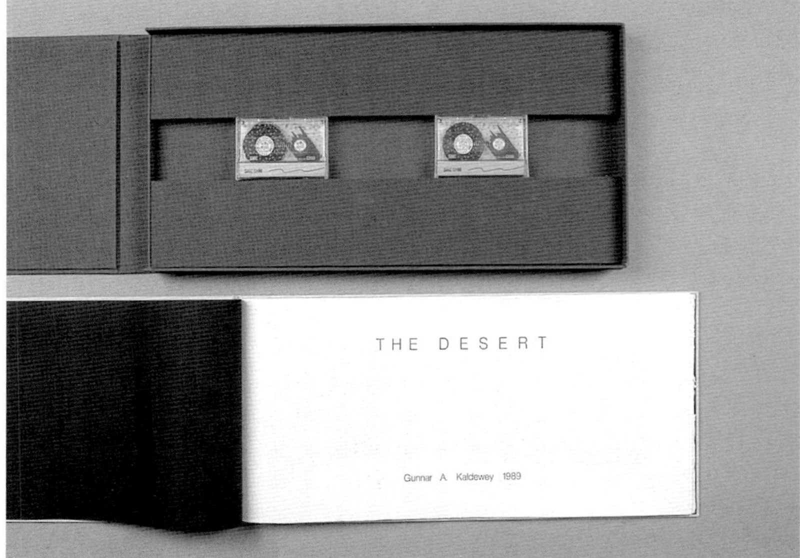

7

Desert.
Sand binding.

Etching for the deluxe edition
on black paper.

Box for the regular edition with
two sound tapes.

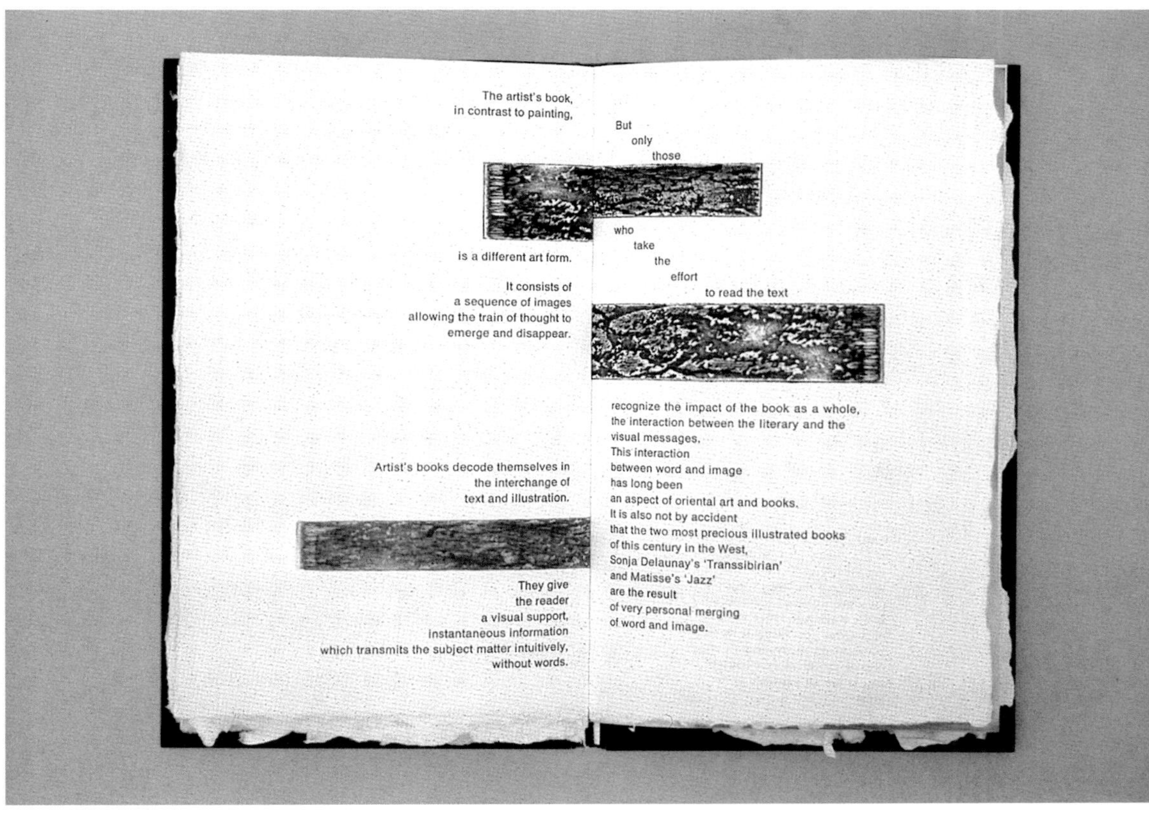

The artist's book,
in contrast to painting,

But
only
those

is a different art form.

It consists of
a sequence of images
allowing the train of thought to
emerge and disappear.

who
take
the
effort
to read the text

recognize the impact of the book as a whole,
the interaction between the literary and the
visual messages.
This interaction
between word and image
has long been
an aspect of oriental art and books.
It is also not by accident
that the two most precious illustrated books
of this century in the West,
Sonja Delaunay's 'Transsibirian'
and Matisse's 'Jazz'
are the result
of very personal merging
of word and image.

Artist's books decode themselves in
the interchange of
text and illustration.

They give
the reader
a visual support,
instantaneous information
which transmits the subject matter intuitively,
without words.

8

Books as Art.

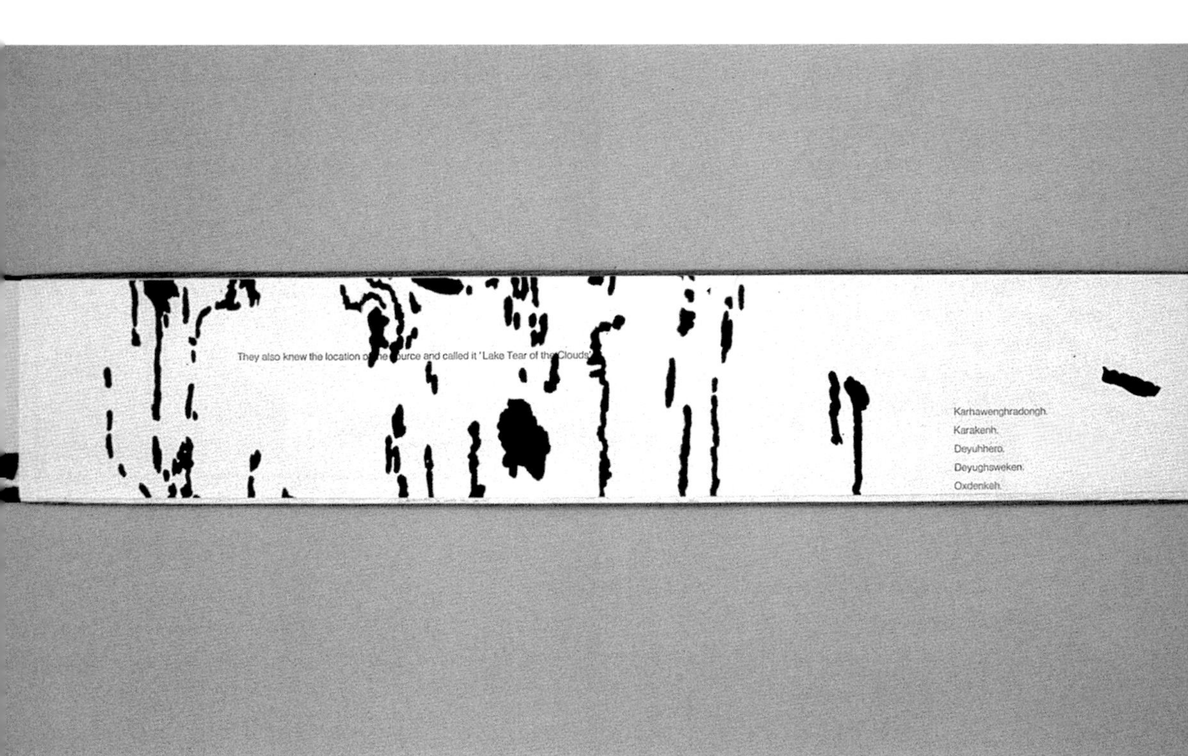

9

Changing waters.
Volume 1: The Hudson River.
Dedicated to John Cage.

10

Changing waters.
Volume 2: Der Rhein.
Leather binding.

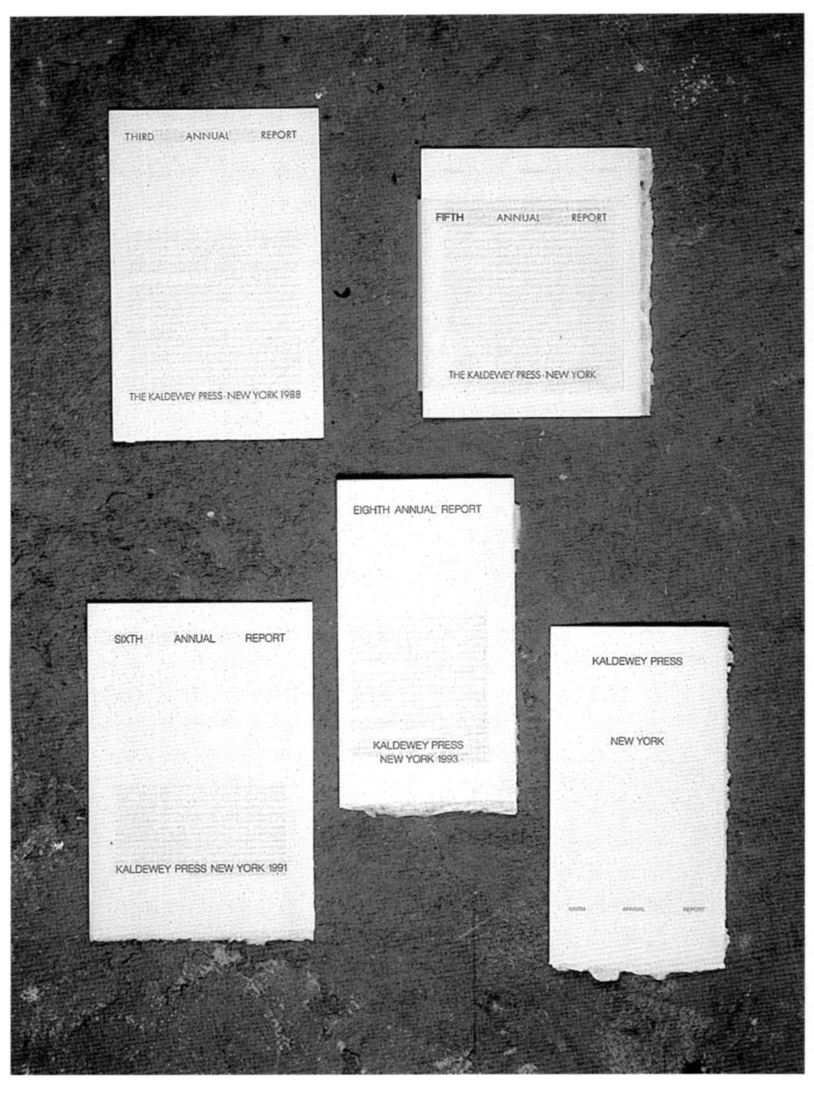

Annual reports

on handmade paper for the
standing order clients of the
Press.

Mindell Dubansky   # The Bookbindings of the Kaldewey Press

In his essay *Books as Art* (**see page 55 + 100**), Gunnar Kaldewey reveals the motivation for the aesthetic of the Kaldewey Press. "It is curiosity about a new text that inspires me to find a new form," Kaldewey writes. "It encourages me to take risks again and again, to find new ways in the use of materials and new conceptions for the aesthetic of the book."

The conceptual elements that inspire Kaldewey are visible in all the remarkable books of the Kaldewey Press. He endeavors to make contemporary books reflect the ideas and materials of the world we live in; and strives to collaborate with an international cadre of writers, artists, and artisans, and encourages their participation in the production of his books. Kaldewey likes as well to experiment with new materials and forms, the better to challenge and delight his readers; and to apply a minimalist approach that helps the natural beauty of a book's materials and structure serve as the primary sources of its decoration.

In the pages below, we'll be looking at how Kaldewey books achieve their remarkable effects, and at the unique and diverse group of binders Kaldewey has assembled to realize their shared visions of the book.

Kaldewey's interest in bookmaking began early. After completing an apprenticeship as a book dealer in Hamburg, he moved to Stuttgart to work in a fine hand bindery that specialized in facsimiles of historic bindings in leather and vellum. During his year at the bench, Kaldewey helped to bind many books. He acquired important hands-on experience, a respect for the craft, and insight into the physical nature of the book.

At the age of twenty-three, Kaldewey founded Antiquariat Kaldewey, and went into business as a rare book dealer. Immediately, he began to collect period bindings, as well as 18th- and 19th-century bookbinding materials and tools, which he used in the restoration of period bindings. For twelve years, Antiquariat Kaldewey supported a bookbinding workshop that employed one full-time binder. Kaldewey, meanwhile, sharpened his eye for and appreciation of well designed and well made books. He became an expert, not only of German and French 18th-century bindings, in which he specialized, but also of European bookbindings in general.

Kaldewey Press books always present an exciting challenge for the printer, binder, and readers. The books are physically complex and often require the skills of talented, experienced binders fo fulfill Kaldewey's desire for elegance and simplicity. Elaborate page materials and formats, as well as the availability of binding materials, will often determine the design of a binding. Kaldewey encourages his artists to be original and free in their work, and relies on the binder's ability to integrate a book's disparate elements into a cohesive, well-functioning package. In the end, it is the binder's contribution that enables readers to experience fully the tactile and sensual qualities of Kaldewey Press books, where colors, textures, scents and sounds work together to guide each reader's perception of the text and illustrations.

Gunnar Kaldewey wants readers to experience his books at a visceral level. He responds to the reader's need for intimacy by requiring that they participate in revealing the pleasures of each book. He does this through the use of transparent, translucent, folded, and cut pages. In addition, cool, reflective, silver-toned metals appear in various formats in several Kaldewey Press books. Metals are a primary material in such books as *Images* (**see page 96**), *In the Beginning...*, Majakowsky's *The Celluloid Heart* (**see page 26**), and *Clouds/Wolken* (**see page 48 + 94**). The fragrant *Trees* and Passolini's, *Ciant da li Ciampanis* are printed on handmade papers made from the bark of cedar trees. These papers, by Japanese papermaker Shusako

Tomi, embody the colors, textures, and coniferous aromas of the trees from which they are made. Sound has always been elemental to Kaldewey's books and sound recordings are a part of several of them. When reading the books, a more subtle use of sound becomes apparent. It is the sound of the book, emanating from the rattle of the pages and the movement of the book.

Kaldewey Press books usually take two years to produce, and some have taken much longer to reach publication. From the beginning of a project, Gunnar Kaldewey plans the materials and bindings that will be used for each book, constantly working to simplify, while bearing in mind the technical strengths and techniques available from the artisans he commissions to bind his books. In these collaborations, Kaldewey's experience, creativity and knowledge of book arts invariably cause his artisans to expand their skills and widen their perceptions about bookmaking. "New and original solutions appear out of technical difficulties and accidents," writes Kaldewey. "Each artist has his own way of solving problems, some work within their technical limits, while other break the rules. In this way the spontaneous and uncalculated style of our books is created."

While Kaldewey usually designs the bindings for Kaldewey Press books, there are several books for which the artists and bookbinders have chiefly designed the bindings. They include the fine edition design bindings of Jean de Gonet, the wooden bindings of Not Vital, and the metal book of Jun Suzuki. In producing the regular and most of the deluxe editions, Kaldewey presents his designs to a binder after the book has been printed. At this point, Kaldewey and the binder enter into a collaboration of making and refining prototypes, until the final choices have been made for binding the different variations of each edition. Sometimes Kaldewey Press editions are published in as many as four bindings, which reflect different perceptions of the text and image relationship. These include *ABC* (see page 49 + 95), Beckett's *Four Poems*, Ashbery's *Not A First* (see page 80) and Passolini's *Ciant da li Ciampanis*. For the regular copies of each edition, Kaldewey's goal is to find the most straightforward, elegant binding. In the deluxe copies he experiments with dynamic, often expensive materials, as well as with adventurous formats and structures.

There are many reasons why Kaldewey's books are so physically challenging to produce. From the start, he experimented with the blending of the traditional and contemporary, as is evident in early books such as *ABC, New York 1977* (see page 46, 47 + 93) and *California Time* (see page 51 + 97). He has used both hand-crafted and industrial materials from all over the world for both the pages and bindings. For pages, Kaldewey often uses combinations of Eastern and Western handmade papers, machine-made papers, synthetic sheets, and such industrial papers as sandpapers, shoemakers "paper" and metallic European "butter paper".

Kaldewey also experiments with the size, shape, and structure of pages; unusually folded and shaped pages often control the reader's access to the text and images. Since they are usually quite large, the pages of the Kaldewey Press books are often printed as separate leaves. When the books are to be bound, rather than presented in a boxed set of loose sheets, it is up to the bookbinder to sew or adhere them together, and make a sound, flexible binding. Books will open the flattest when they have been sewn through the fold; and to transform the individual pages into folded gatherings, the pages need to be "guarded" together. This procedure entails pasting thin strips of paper, usually japanese tissue, to attach the leaves together. This can be a difficult task when the book is large and the two leaves are off different sizes and materials, as the Kaldewey Press books often are.

After the leaves of a book have been attached by sewing or adhesive, the binder makes the cover or "case." Kaldewey Press books are covered in a great variety of materials, including paper, vellum, traditional and fashion leathers, textiles, wood, and metal; and they assume a variety of shapes, includ-ing round, triangular, cylindrical, and exaggerated rectangular shapes. On these covers, Kaldewey experiments with a variety of surface textures and decorative techniques, including painted paper and leather, the application of sand, and blind and metallic stamping.

It is standard for each Kaldewey Press book to be delivered in an enclosure to give the book a measure of protection. These enclosures take various traditional and non-traditional forms. The most common style of box used by the Kaldewey Press is the chemise and slipcase. Kaldewey Press slipcases are covered in gray Canson paper with titles stamped on the spine. Most regular editions come in these, as do other thin books which lack three-dimensional or fragile surfaces. Traditional cloth-covered drop-spine boxes are made for large or complex bindings; and wooden and metal enclosures are sometimes used when required by the design of the book.

As the desire to take risks is intrinsic to the philosophy of the Kaldewey Press, Kaldewey and his collaborators often push the physical book to its limits. Thus, even though their concepts may have seemed strong, there are occasional failures in the design of the structure or the compatibility of materials which result in a physical weakness in the binding. There are only two books where this would be obvious to non-binders. One is the beautiful stainless steel binding for *Clouds/Wolken* (**see page 48 + 94**): The piano hinge binding opens perfectly flat, but the adhesive that attaches the textblock to the binding has failed in every copy I have seen. The other is the deluxe version of *The Desert* (**see page 54**), bound by BookLab, in which actual desert sand that has been mixed with an adhesive, covers the entire binding. The sand mixture should not have been glued to the joints, since pieces break off when the book is opened.

Even though such technical risks have not always paid off, Kaldewey's willingness to take risks has reaped many successes and the great majority of the Kaldewey Press books are technically exquisite. The binding that Kaldewey feels works most harmoniously with the text and which is therefore, one of the most successful, is the regular edition of Kafka's *Der Prozess* (**see page 37**), bound by Christian Zwang. *Der Prozess* is printed and bound using the same soft, natural Chinese paper. The paper is adhered to the boards only at the turn-ins, allowing the natural beauty of the sheet to dominate and contribute to the flexibility of the volume, which is decorated with only a small paper title label.

The bindings, boxes, and enclosures for Kaldewey Press books have been made by many fine binders and craftspeople. The binders include Christian, Thomas, and Burkhart Zwang in Hamburg; Jean de Gonet in Paris; Cornelia Ahnert in Chemnitz; BookLab, Inc. in Austin, Texas, and Lobstein in Paris. Boxes and enclosures have been made by Judi Conant in Vermont, Atelier Dermont-Duval in Paris, Nello Nanni in New York, and Shahin Cabinetmaker in Albany.

Christian Zwang, Hamburg

In many ways, the fine edition bindings made by Christian Zwang and Sons, who have bound the majority of the Kaldewey Press books, are responsible for creating the elegant look of Kaldewey Press books. They are among the most beautiful and well made bindings of their kind, and set the standard of quality for other Kaldewey Press binders.

Christian Zwang comes from several generations of bookbinders. His father, Friedrich, studied in Berlin with Paul Kersten, one of the leading fine binders of his time. Kersten bound elaborate period and facsimile bindings, as well as others in the style of the Arts and Crafts movement. After leaving Berlin, Friedrich Zwang settled in Dresden and opened his own binding workshop, which was destroyed in the bombing of 1945.

Christian learned bookbinding from Friedrich and an older brother, Theophil, by working in their new bindery at the Dresden Academy of Fine Arts from 1947 through 1950. Christian was fortunate to have had his father for a teacher, and to have lived at a time when legendary artists and craftsmen worked on fine bookbindings. While working at the Academy of Fine Arts, Christian also had the opportunity to meet artists Otto Dix and Josef Hegenbarth, whose influence would make a fundamental and lasting impression on his work.

From 1954 to 1956, Christian studied bookbinding with Kurt Londenberg, at the fine arts school, Hochschule Am Lerchenfeld, in Hamburg. Londenberg had been the protege of the great binder, Ignaz Wiemeler. Through Londenberg, Christian learned the techniques of fine craft bookbinding. At Lerchen-feld, he also met the typographer, Richard von Sichowsky and the private press printer Otto Rohse, who would become important clients and friends. In 1956, Christian set up a bindery with Theophil. They worked together for two years, after which Theophil departed. Christian continued the workshop on his own. Through the years, Christian has been fortunate to have clients such as Sichowsky, Rohse, the fine press publisher Roswitha Quadflieg, the publisher Ernst Hauswedell, and, of course, Gunnar Kaldewey. Since the 1970's, Christian Zwang has been regarded by his peers as the lead-ing fine edition binder in Ger-many. The binding styles he has developed are uniquely his own, and radically different from traditional fine bindings.

The relationship between Kaldewey and Christian Zwang began in 1969 when Kaldewey, still in his rare book business, purchased an early Zwang binding and became inspired by its quality and the graceful fit of the slipcase. Shortly after, Kaldewey travelled to Hamburg to meet Zwang, and in 1976, when he printed his first book, Kaldewey was anxious to collaborate with Zwang on the binding. This book was *Grimond de la Renière* (see page 7 + 45), which Kaldewey produced for members of his male cooking club. Its design combined Kaldewey's and Zwang's mutual interest in, and talent for, making books that were thin, flexible, and elegant. *Grimond de la Renière* is skillfully bound in a flat-back paper case, using very thin boards which have been blind-stamped with perfection. Since the beginning, their relationship has continued unbroken, with Kaldewey constantly challenging Zwang's skills and imagination in ways that generate wonderful results. To date, the Zwang workshop has produced forty-three different bindings for twenty-five Kaldewey editions. Christian Zwang retired from the bookbinding bench in 1993, leaving his business to his sons, Thomas and Burkhart, who both served apprenticeships with their father. Thomas directs the workshop, where he and Burkhart work together with their staff, and continue to bind books for the Kal-dewey Press. Fine-edition binding is only a part of their business, they also repair and rebind books for libraries and private collectors, and manage an art gallery.

Few people have had the luxury to spend time alone with and handle the Kaldewey/Zwang books, although quite a few are available to the public at the Spencer Collection in the New York Public Library. It is only by spending time alone with the books, and not through the glare of an exhibition case, or in photo-graphic reproductions, that the books can be fully seen and appreciated. A successful binding begins with a philosophy of structure, a plan that begins with the folding of the pages, and follows the book through its sewing, backing, and covering – each element contributing to the total book. For Christian Zwang, the beauty of a binding is not necessarily related to the use of precious materials, or to very complicated bind-ing techniques; it is more the spirit of the book's text, which gives the book its form. Zwang sees himself as a craftsman, and feels his work should serve the arts. His bindings always compliment the texts with their simplicity and structural lightness, by the textures and colors of his materials, and by the compatibility of titling and decoration. Zwang bindings are remarkable for their taste and precision. Carefully selected and prepared materials, including covering materials, endleaves, binders' board, lining papers, and adhesives, all contribute to the aesthetic and physical quality of Zwang bindings (see page 23, 29, 34, 49, 57, 80, 81, 84, 95, 100

+ 101). This is craftmanship at its best, a level where one can't always determine why the object is so right, but one knows that it is. Even if other binders could analyze the elements of Zwang's work, I doubt many could reproduce them with his success.

All of the Zwang bindings are a pleasure to look at and to handle. A few appeal especially strongly to me because of their sensitivity to the book's contents, the beauty of their proportions, the colors, the textures, the scent; and their level of craftsmanship. Ma favorite Zwang binding is the bold, red morroco deluxe binding with sparkling silver stamping on *On the Marionette Theater of Heinrich von Kleist,* designed by Elaine Cohen (see page 81). I believe this binding and the one for Kafka's *Der Prozess* (see page 37) are two of Zwang's and Kaldewey's greatest successes. They are pure of design and are compatible with their fascinating texts.

There are other Kaldewey/Zwang collaborations that are extremely engaging. These include the deluxe version of *Trees* (see page 53), which is made from naturally scented handmade cedar paper and bound in a snakeskin-embossed paper with embossed calf inlays; the painted calfskin binding on *Song of Songs* (see page 84); and the blind-embossed paper binding for the regular version of Beckett's, *Quatre Poemes.*

Jean de Gonet, Paris

The work of artist and bookbinder Jean de Gonet is unique in the world of twentieth-century fine bookbinding, and Gunnar Kaldewey is fortunate to possess the only fine press for which de Gonet has designed and bound editions. In his bindings, art and craft combine to create objects of wonder and beauty. The two de Gonet edition bindings on Kaldewey Press books are the deluxe bindings for Beckett's *Quatre Poemes* and Duras' *Hiroshima Mon Amour.* They are among the press' most original and compelling books, and are the only Kaldewey Press bookbindings designed by a bookbinder. Kaldewey met de Gonet in 1986, while de Gonet was organizing an exhibition of his work at the Center for Book Arts in New York City. During this period, de Gonet often travelled from Paris and occasionally stayed in Kaldewey's New York City home where he studied the books of the Kaldewey Press. Finding them to his liking, he agreed to design and bind deluxe editions of future publications.

De Gonet learned about bookbinding and the book arts while he was in college. Immediately, he became enmeshed in the craft. Although largely self-taught, he received technical training in the bookbindery of the Service de la Marine from 1971 to 1975, after which he began founded his own workshop. Like Zwang, de Gonet reacted against traditional French fine binding structures and designs, which are characterized by inflexible structures, a profusion of gold-tooling, and leather mosaic decoration.

In 1977, de Gonet began to create new binding structures which were inspired by the nature of his materials and by the infrastructure of the binding. Jean de Gonet does not make case bindings; all of his bindings are made on the book. He always reveals a book's sewing structure by making a slotted leather spine which exposes the sewing supports. He embellishes these supports, which can be leather thongs or linen cords, be sewing his books with black linen thread, and then lacing the ends of the supports into the boards, creating a strong cover to text attachment. De Gonet uses the area of the covers, where the supports are laced in, to draw the viewer's attention by subtle decorative elements that are reminiscent of structural elements of medieval and Renaissance bindings. For example, he may use tiny metal fasteners or wooden pegs to simulate the anchoring in of the cords, or blind-tooling to accentuate this area.

De Gonet is known for developing several types of cover treatments for his unique and edition bindings. They are characterized by unusual leather-working techniques, reticulated wooden bindings, and industrial plastic or *Revorim* bindings. De Gonet works with bookbinding and fashion leathers, and explores a variety of dying, distressing, tooling, stamping, and other surface-altering techniques. He manipulates the skins and utilizes their natural colors, textures, irregularities, and blemishes.

Hiroshima Mon Amour (see page 75) is a showcase of these techniques. It is a flexible leather splitskin binding. A laminate of thick leather and paper replaces binder's board. Angled hardwood spine supports and galvanized steel foredge supports give rigidity and weight to the covers. Because the book has complex folding pages, paper stubs are attached to the spine edge of the pages and the book is stab-sewn in the Japanese style. Although the binding is deceivingly simple, it reveals upon close inspection finely crafted details that are both functional and decorative. These details include grooves cut into the front surface of the wooden spine pieces to cradle and protect the sewing threads, tiny pegs that lock the ends of the threads into the wooden spinepiece, minature red leather inlays which nest inside the rivets that attach the steel foredge strips to the covers, and a running stitch that sews the leather and endpapers together at the head and tail of the covers.

The deluxe version of Beckett's *Quatre Poems* (see page 77) is an example of de Gonet's flexible, reticulated, lightweight wooden bindings. De Gonet has adhered eight narrow vertical slats of stained hardwood to a textile backing on each cover of the book's triangular binding. The binding is punctuated with ebony foredge tips, with blind-tooled leather onlays, and other unique finishing techniques. The panels on the front cover are stained green and the back panels are stained red, reflecting the colors in which the English and French tests are printed.

Collaborations with other workshops

Cornelia Ahnert is the most recent fine edition binder to collaborate on the books of the Kaldewey Press. Like Christian Zwang, Ahnert's ancestors were bookbinders, and it is through them that she gained her early experience and insights into the world of the book. Ahnert's grandfather was a binder for the trade, and her father, who learned his craft in Dresden, owned his own bookbinding business for over thirty years. Ahnert earned her diploma in designer bookbinding, in Halle/Burg Giebichenstein, at the School of Art and Design, where she was able to explore her interests through papermaking, drawing, printing, printmaking, and bookmaking. In 1990, while still a student, Ahnert purchased a book bindery in Chemnitz from a retiring binder.

Ahnert shares with all of the Kaldewey Press binders a love of experimentation, practical functionality, and a respect for the natural beauty of materials. In creating an edition, Ahnert says that her aim is "First, to find the spirit of the book and then, to transport this spirit out of the book on to the cover. I do this by using the special technical know-how of a bookbinder along with the freedom of choice in colors, materials, scripts, shapes, etc. of a designer or an artist."

Gunnar Kaldewey met Ahnert in 1991, at his booth at the Frankfurt Book Fair. After showing Kaldewey photographs of her work, he was so impressed that he soon visited her Chemnitz studio. Ahnert appreciates the simplicity and generosity of Kaldewey's books and share's his philosophy, especially in that she also desires to collaborate with others in the creating beautiful and contemporary works. During the meeting in Chemnitz, Ahnert showed Kaldewey several binding designs and was pleased when a short time later, he asked her to design a binding for the Kaldewey Press. Ahnert has since bound three editions for the Kaldewey Press: both regular and deluxe editions of Ovid's, *Metamorphosibus Historia Apollinis et Daphnes;* both editions of Walter Benjamin's, *Angelus Novus;* and Paul Celan's, *Sand aus den Urnen.*

Ahnert's bindings are elegant and well made. She strives for perfection. These qualities can be seen at their best in her triple-binding for the Ovid/Caponegro book in which her collaboration with Kaldewey yields striking results. Kaldewey's inspiration for this triptych came from the late sculptural work of Isamu Noguchi. In this work, Noguchi cut stones in several pieces and put them together again. To Kaldewey, East meets West in these cut-stone sculptures, in an international style that is also inherent to the Kaldewey Press books.

The Ovid/Caponegro book (see page 38 + 86) is constructed in three parts; the original Latin text, its new English version, and a colophon volume. When Kaldewey visited Ahnert, he admired her technique for making "paper strip" bindings and asked her to bind the Ovid in this style. These are flat-back case bindings. The covers are made from colored paper strips in blue, green, and yellow laid across each other at right angles. The strips are pasted around the edges of the covers onto the insides of the boards, where they disappear under the endpapers. A sheet of blue paper is pasted over the strips, leaving only the edges exposed. Then this paper is scored with great precision to accentuate the thickness of the papers below. A little wooden strip locks the books into perfect alignment, while resting in their box. These books can best be appreciated when seen in raking light.

A very different but equally successful binding is the deluxe edition of Benjamin's *Angelus Novus* (see page 7). This simple, yet bold design was inspired by the boldness of the woodcuts by the artist Heribert Ottersbach. The binding is a contemporary version of an Asian stab-sewn binding. The book is printed on flexible Chinese paper and the pages have been folded on the foredge. The book is bound in two large pieces of unfinished natural calfskin, which were lined with black Japanese paper and cut flush; the binding is held together by five large chrome grommets.

In keeping with his desire to collaborate with an international group of craftspeople, Gunnar Kaldewey selected the American bindery, BookLab, Inc., in Austin, Texas, to bind the deluxe versions of Broaddus' *Sphinx and the Bird of Paradise* (see page 69) and *The Desert* (see page 54). BookLab is large hand bookbindery that predominantly binds limited-edition books, and also makes boxes and photocopies of books for libraries and small presses. Founded in 1984 by Craig Jensen, BookLab seeks to fill a gap in the American hand bookbinding and bookmaking industry. Its goal is to offer publishers and libraries, fairly priced, high quality bindings and enclosures that are superior in materials, design, and fabrication to those of other commercial library and edition binderies. Jensen began his bindery with one employee in his garage. Today, BookLab employs thirty staffers who occupy 13,000 square feet of space.

BookLab's first Kaldewey Press project is the deluxe version of John Eric Broaddus' unfinished Xerographic book, *Sphinx and the Bird of Paradise.* The book was bound in leather, using the case-making style of Christian Zwang as a model. *The Desert* must have been a challenge to BookLab staff. The binding they created interprets the book's text literally. It is bound in a white cloth case binding. After binding, sand was adhered to the entire binding, giving the reader a feeling for the environment that inspired the book.

Among traditional materials, Kaldewey enjoys using wood and metal. He feels that wood is a natural material for bookmaking. With the exception for the Gonet's *Quatre Poems bindings,* all the wooden boxes and covers for Kaldewey Press books have been made by Shahin Cabinetmaking, in Albany, New York, which is near the Kaldewey Press in Poestenkill. The two firms enjoy working together and share a long history of collaboration. Shahin Kasparian, with his father, Nisan, and brother, Arjante, specialize in making fine wooden inlays and fretwork for guitars and other musical instruments. The Kasparian family, itself, is Armenian, from Turkey, and has lived in the New York area for almost twenty-five years. Their Kaldewey projects include the Russian birch boards and yellow pine slipcase for the editions of the Pasolini/Vital book *Ciant de li Ciampanis* (see page 30 + 31); followed by the ebony covers for *Books as Art* (see page 100), the Brazilian rosewood spine pieces and Japanese-style box for *Trees* (see page 10 + 98). Recently, Shahin Cabinetmaking made the wooden box for Kaldewey Press' first multiple, *By an Earthquake, by John Ashbery and David Ireland* (see page 88). As in most Kaldewey's collaborations with bookbinders, Kaldewey provides rough drawings. Shahin then makes a prototype, changes are made, and the work is completed.

Artists' bindings: Jun Suzuki, Richard Tuttle and Not Vital

Some of the most innovative bindings on Kaldewey Press books are the sculptural books designed by artists. These are the metal book of Jun Suzuki, the deluxe edition of Richard Tuttle's *The Gyres (Source of Imagery)* and Not Vital's elephant-folio edition of Pasolini's *Ciant di la Ciampanis*. These books move towards Gunnar Kaldewey's idea of creating the "global book," in which aesthetics from different cultures merge, enabling people from diverse cultural backgrounds to understand the book. The "global book" transcends language and speaks to the intuitive nature of the reader. In Kaldewey's view of the contemporary book, all of the elements of the book, including paper, text, printing, illustration, binding, and movement, combine to communicate the idea of the book to the reader.

Jun Suzuki is a sculptor who uses metal and stone in his work. His book, *In the Beginning...* (see page 24 + 25), is about the creation of language. *In the Beginning...* is cut from twelve sheets of galvanized steel. Each sheet contains a silk-screened Japanese text with an English translation stencilled and cut-out of the sheet. The text consists of words which describe physical activities utilized in the creation of speech. On the last page, printed on Japanese paper, is the first sentence of known Japanese text. Suzuki has altered the metal pages by the application of rice vinegar so that the appearance of the book would change over time.

Not Vital has always felt a connection with early and ethnic books and has looked to them for inspiration in his work. The natural materials and forms of these books appeal to him. Vital enjoys pushing the technical limits of this books through the use of large and unwieldy forms and unusual materials.

For the binding of Pasolini's *Ciant da li Ciampanis* (see page 30, 31, 78 + 79), Vital designed a massive sculptural wooden binding with metal hinges in the shape of Pasta da L'ov, egg cookies, which are a traditional dish from the Engadine of Switzerland (see page 30). The concept for this binding was clear to him at the beginning of his collaboration with Kaldewey. In contrast, his deluxe binding for *Confucius: The Great Learning* was inspired by the text and its design grew out of the making of the book. The binding of woven branches, twigs and grasses represents an oriental-style gift and is a continuation of the Vital's illustrations, in which a continuous line travels through the text, wrapping around similar Chinese characters.

For Richard Tuttle, the book has a flow, an interior energy, which results from the interaction of the folding of the paper, the images and the text. In Tuttle's concept of the contemporary book, the page is seen as sculptural media and he seeks "to find space on the page" through the process of creating the book. He is intrigued by the way in which the terminology and symmetry of the book relates to the human body and human condition – spine, head, gutter. Tuttle is looking for something new in bookmaking; and it is through his participation in the production of the book that the possibility for unforseen ideas are brought about and he is able to be open to the process.

In, *Gyres (Source of Imagery)*, (see page 43 + 90 + 91), Tuttle wanted to transform traditional arrangements of text and images into something original. The book is bound by Thomas Zwang, in full flexible black calf-skin, with no decoration or stamping. A single doublure on the front cover pays homage to the traditional book. In the center of the doublure, a small square is cut out of the board revealing the soft, reverse side of the covering leather. The cut-out is bordered by an inlay of vermillion and gold-leafed paper. The fly-leaves are plain black Japanese paper and the pages are constructed of two long rectangular sheets of paper, laminated perpendicularly and folded once to create the illusion of a square. The transluscent fold-out pages create a continuous circuit of alternating opaqueness and transparency throughout the book.

Gunnar Kaldewey will continue to explore the world of bookmaking. He will encourage and collaborate with artists and craftspeople from the international community, and he will continue to experiment with innovative materials and book structures.

List of illustrations

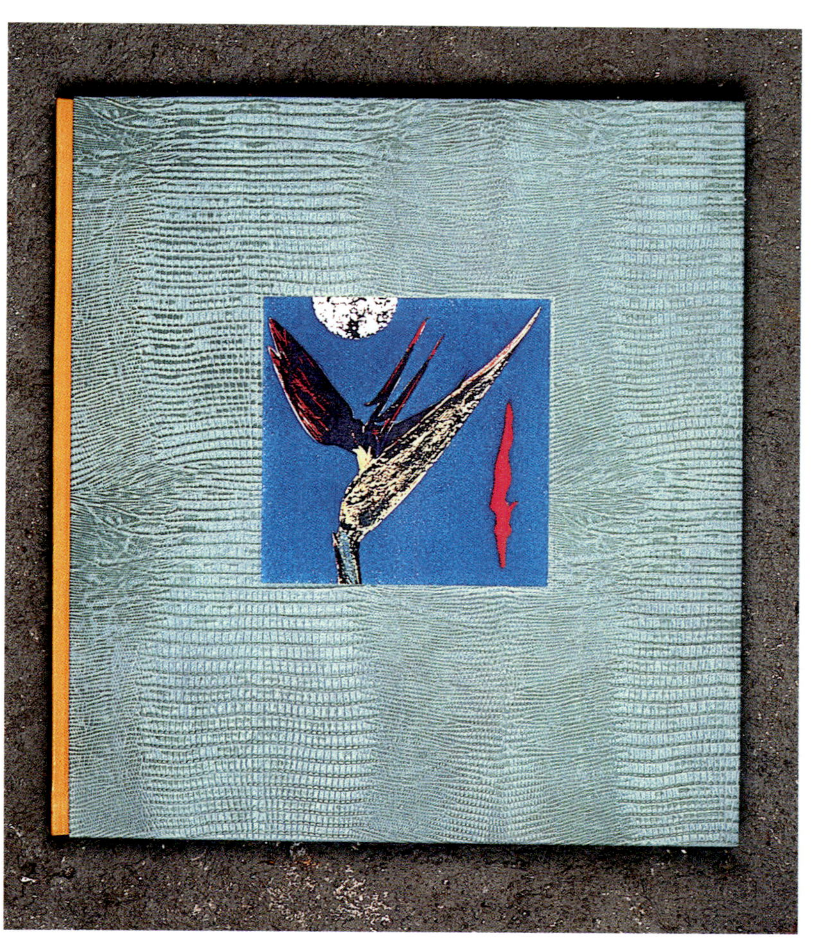

3

John Eric Broaddus,
Sphinx and the Bird of Paradise.

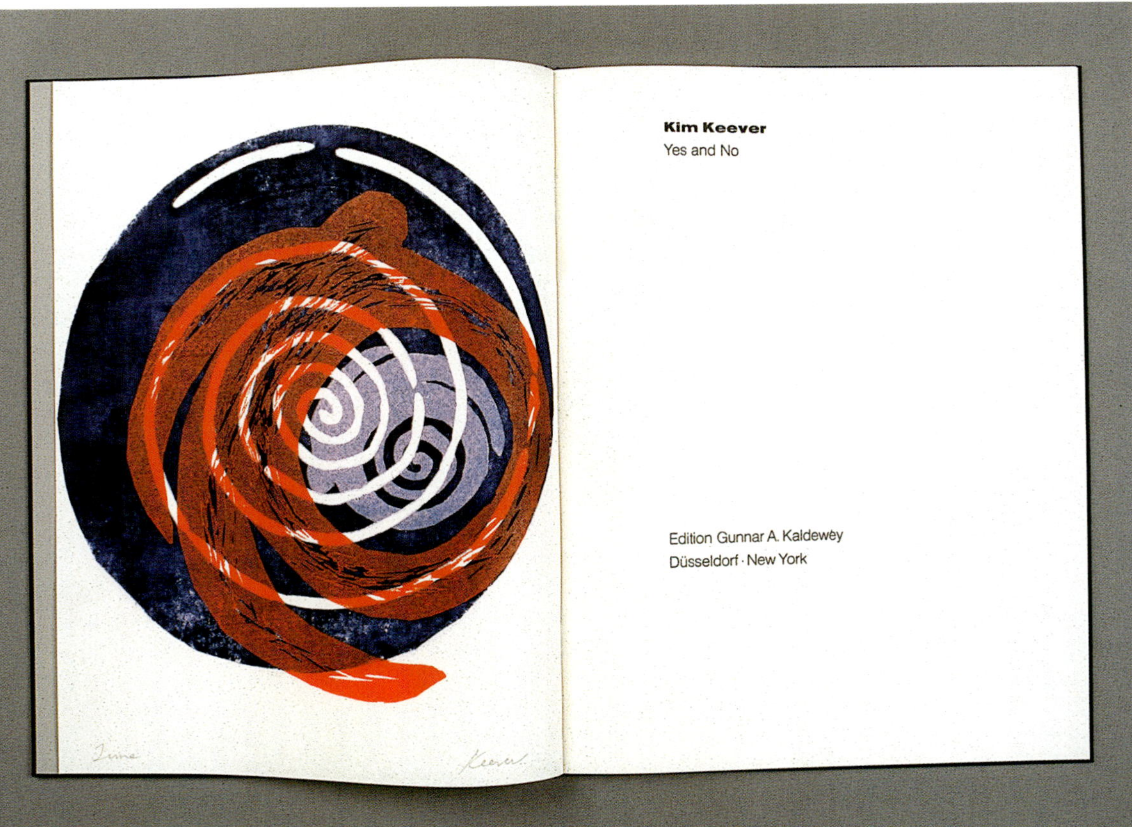

4

Kim Keever, Yes and No.

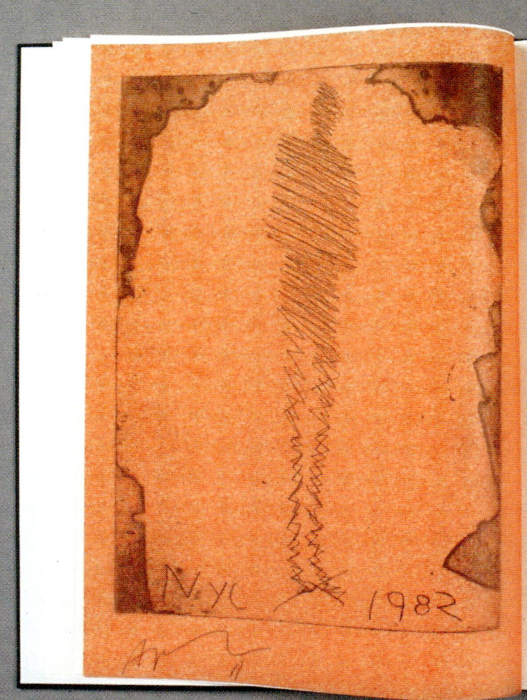

William Burroughs

Mummies

with etchings

by Carl Apfelschnitt

Edition Gunnar A. Kaldewey

Düsseldorf · New York

1982

5

William Burroughs, Mummies.
Etching by Carl Apfelschnitt.

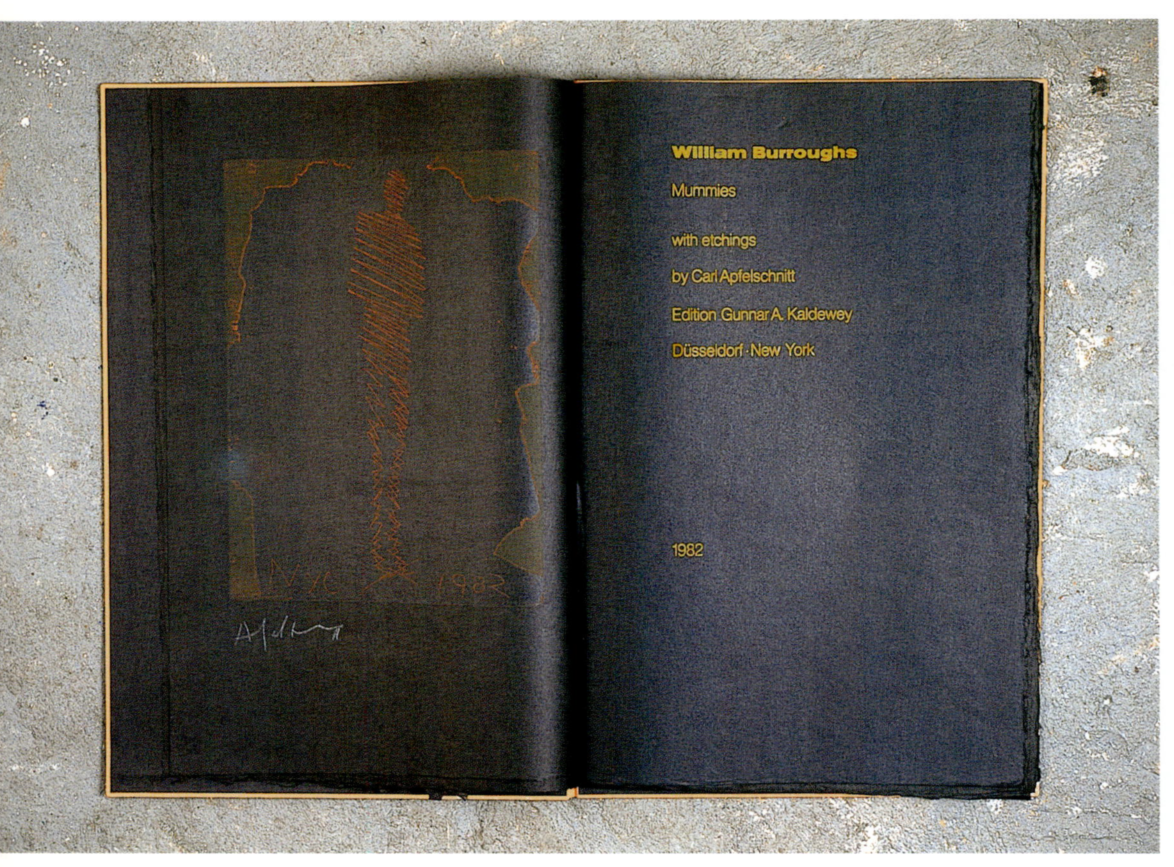

5

Mummies.
Deluxe edition. Printed in gold
on black Japanese paper.

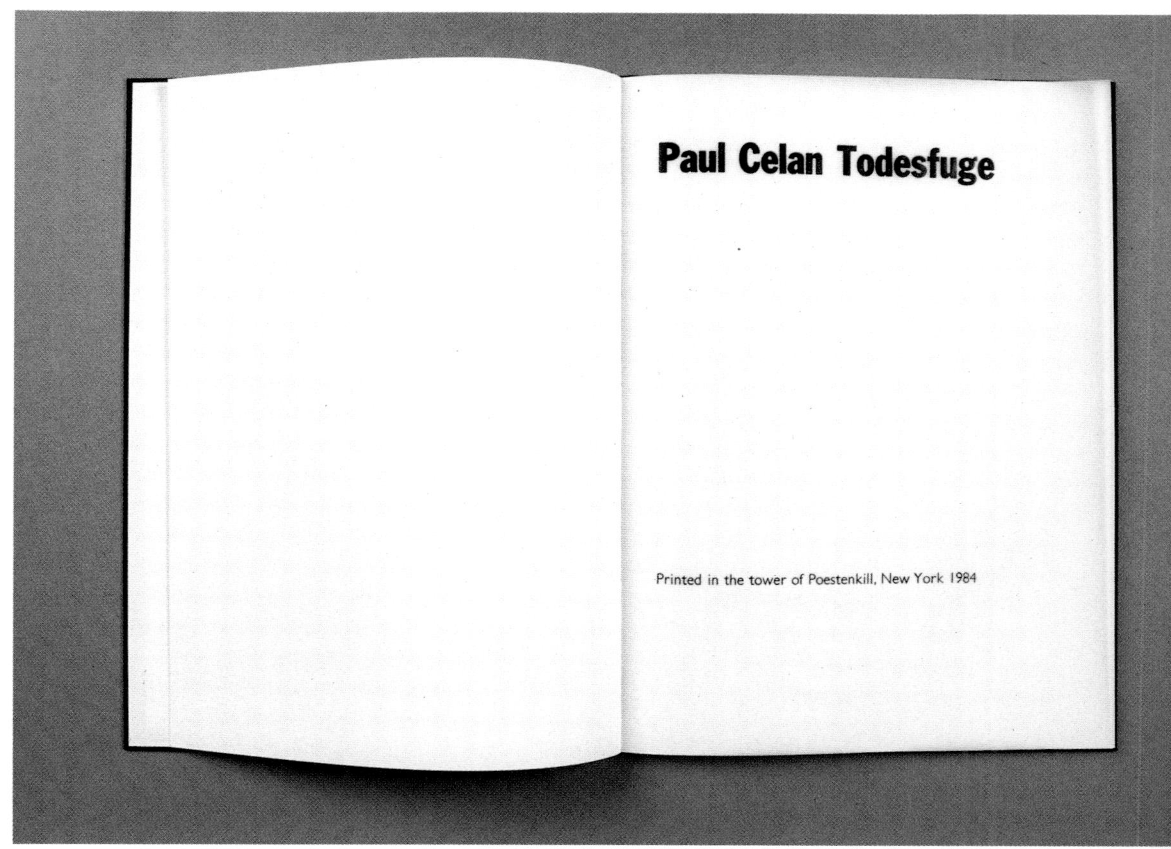

9

Paul Celan, Todesfuge.
Paper cuts by Mischa Kuball.

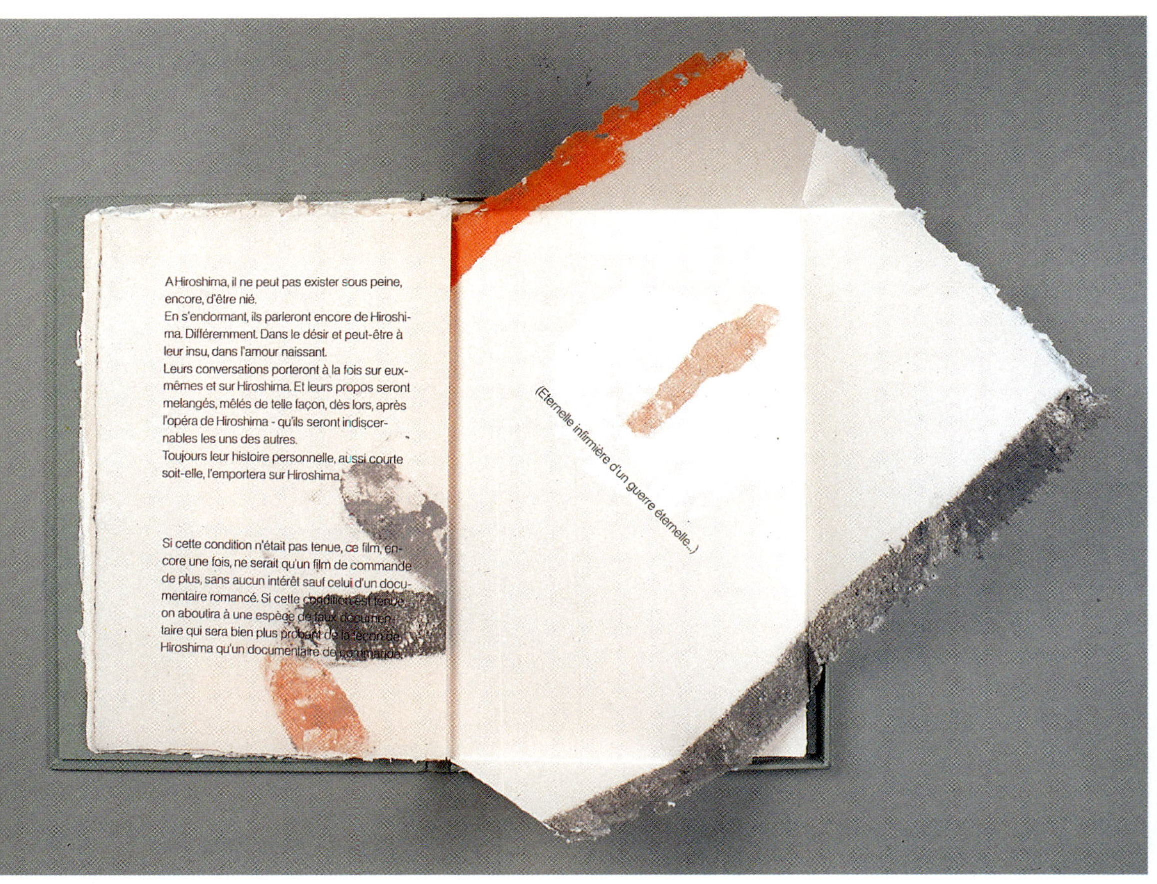

10

Marguerite Duras,

Hiroshima Mon Amour.

Paper pulp images by
Ann Sperry.

Hiroshima Mon Amour.
Jean de Gonet binding.

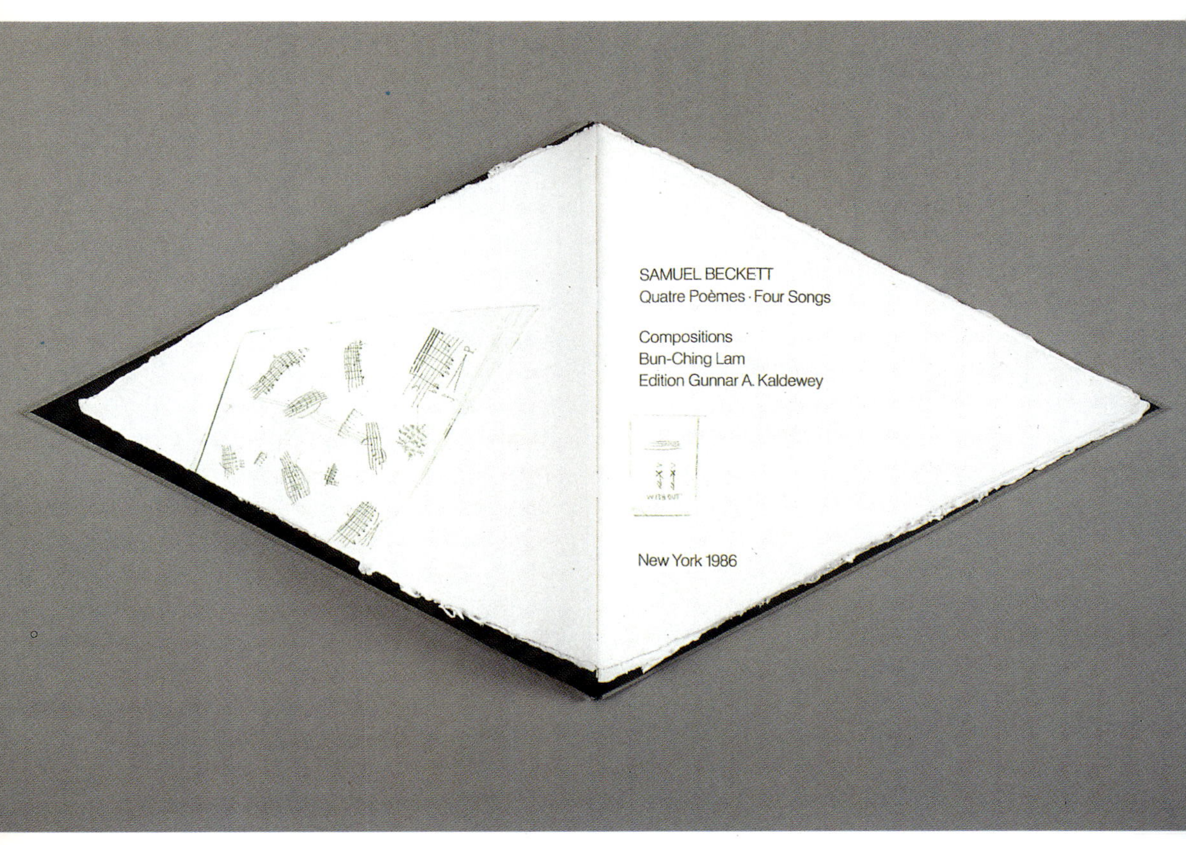

11

Samuel Beckett.

Quatre poèmes.

Title page.

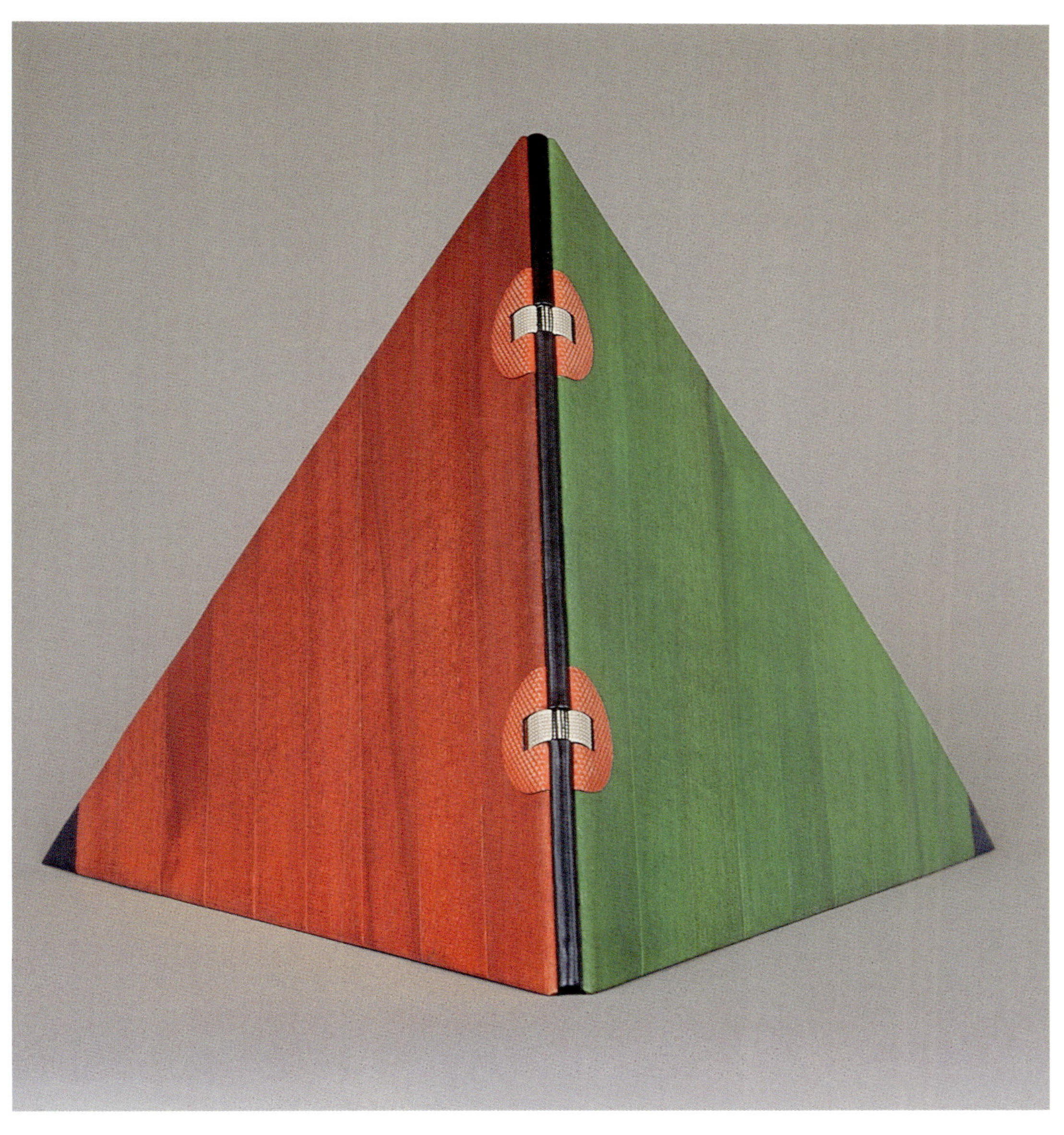

Quatre Poèmes.
Jean de Gonet wooden
binding.

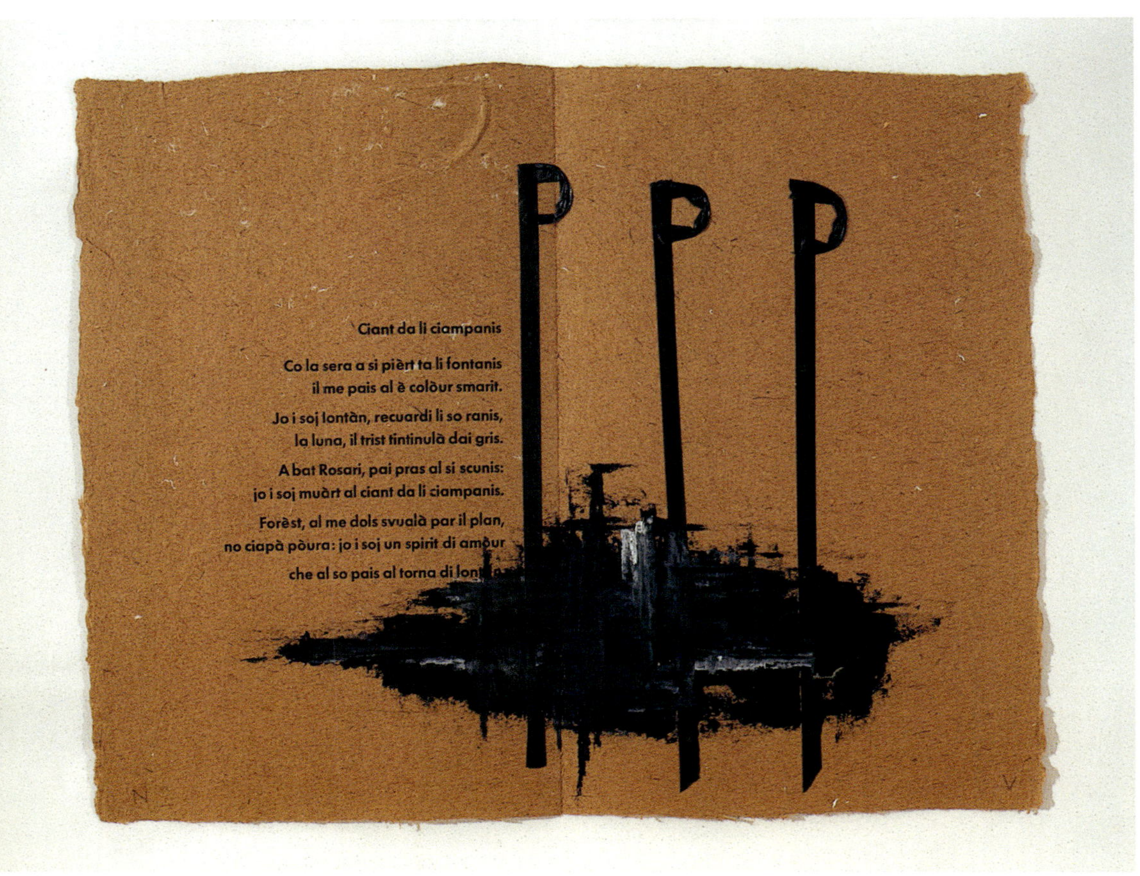

12

Pier Paolo Pasolini,

Ciant da li ciampanis.

Original drawing by Not Vital.

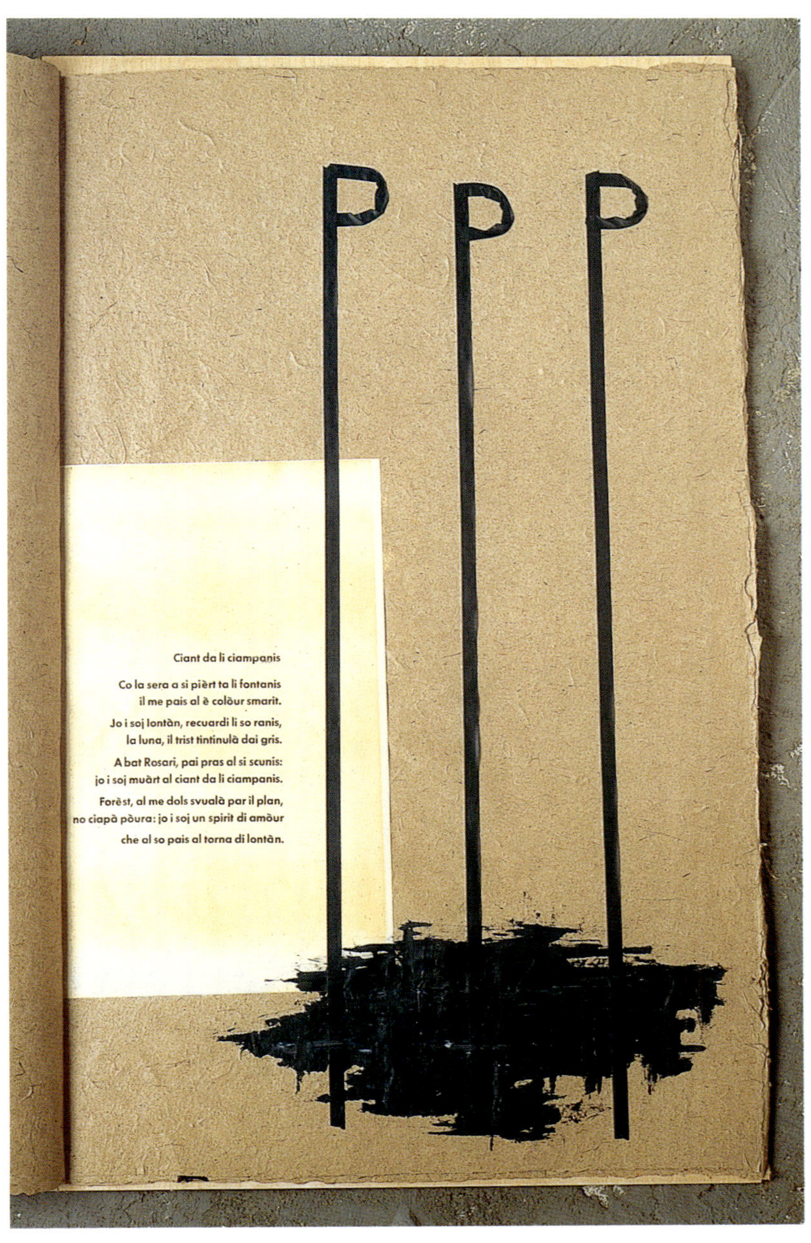

Not Vital,

Poesias rumantschas.

Pasolini page for the elephant
folio edition.

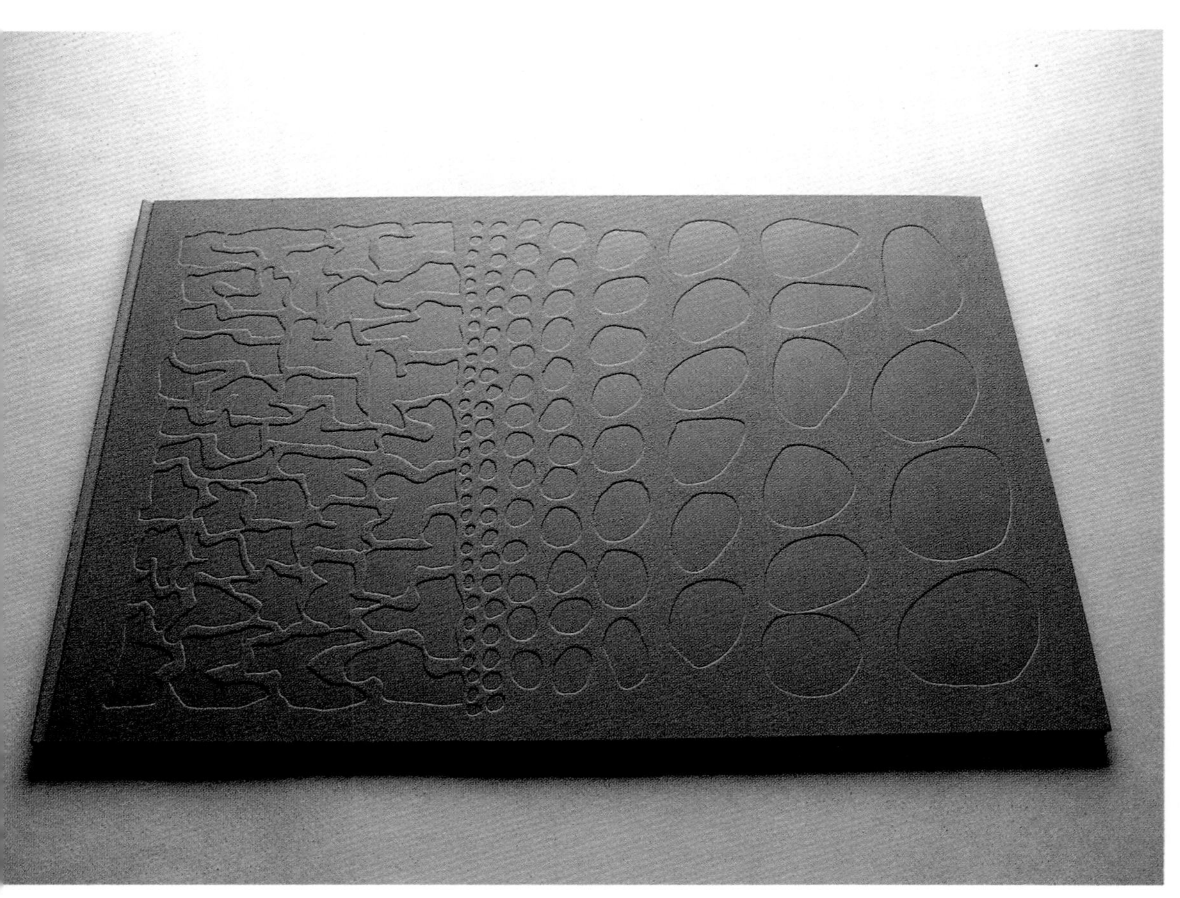

13

John Ashbery, Not a First.
Paper over board binding,
relief print after a design by
Jonathan Lasker.

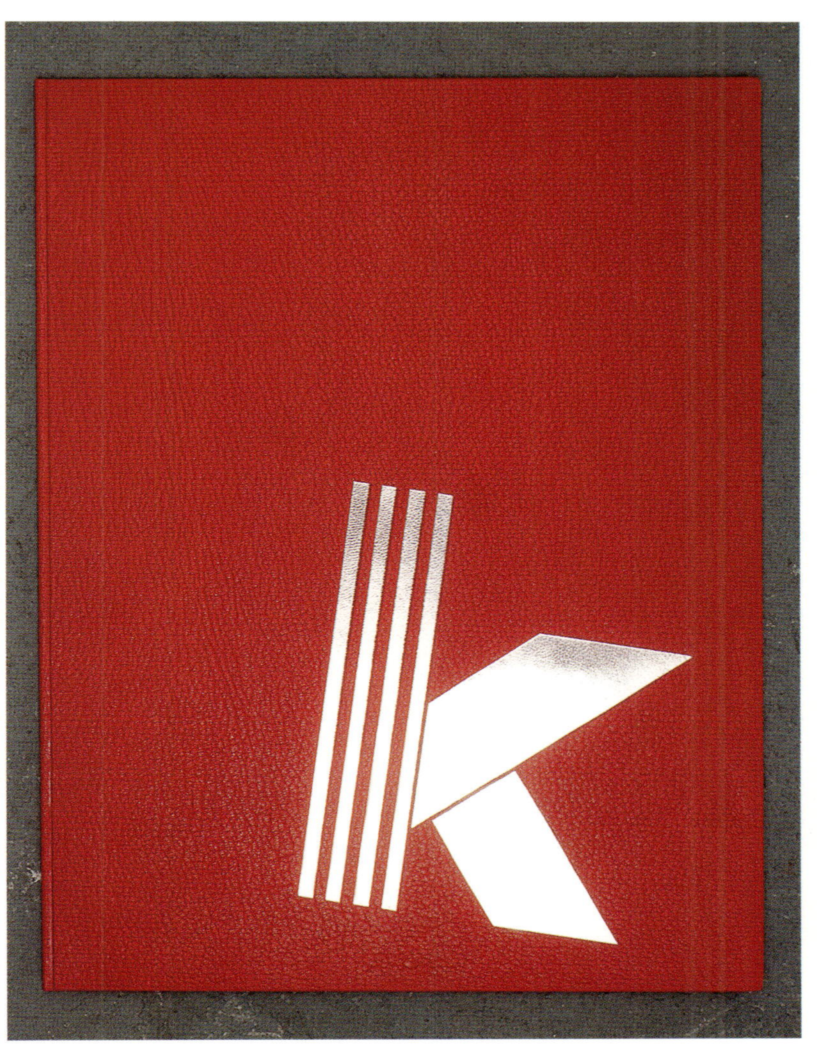

14

Arthur A. Cohen,
The Marionette Theater
of Heinrich von Kleist.
Morocco binding designed by
Elaine Lustig Cohen.

theory of knowledge. Kleist steps back from the Kantian abyss (not a retreat into »dogmatic slumber«), and a new theoria grounded upon a metaphysics of the unconscious, the creative, and the grace that proceeds from art.

A word about the title. The essay might have been called more simply, more directly, more objectively über die Marionetten, about the marionettes. But Kleist does not choose simplicity. Even though he speaks of the marionette theater as a spectacle set up for public recreation, the dialogue that ensues does not deal with the ensemble playing of the marionettes except in the course of reference to Teniers. That reading is dismissed as a mere appearance of painterly beauty on the first half page. Obviously the »theater« is the universe and the marionettes are world-players who will unfold to us -- through the masterfull exegesis of the dancer -- the wisdom their wood conceals. Note as well that although published only ten months before his suicide, Kleist had dated »his« encounter the winter of 1801, that is precisely at the time of his famous »Kant crisis.«

The most remarkble omission in Heinrich von Kleist's extrodinary essay concerning the marionette theater is that never once does he speak about the marionette manipulator, the master of marionettes, the shadowy personage behind the perfect grace of the dancing figures. It is not, of course, that Kleist forgot anything. He omitted nothing from his little essay, except of course those elements that make an essay a proper, conventional essay. There is no systematic exposition, no argument from beginning to end. Quite the contrary, all conclusions are set forth at the beginning. As the suite of conversations and narratives proceed the conclusions already described are settled deeper and deeper into the unconscious dreaming of the race. Clearly no need then for the deepest of pessimists to admit that God is better at manipulating marionettes than he is at conducting human beings. The hidden hand of marionette grace is graceless in his bounties towards his most miserable creation.
Arthur A. Cohen, 1985

14

Arthur A. Cohen,

On the Marionette Theater.

woodcuts and typography
by Elaine Lustig Cohen

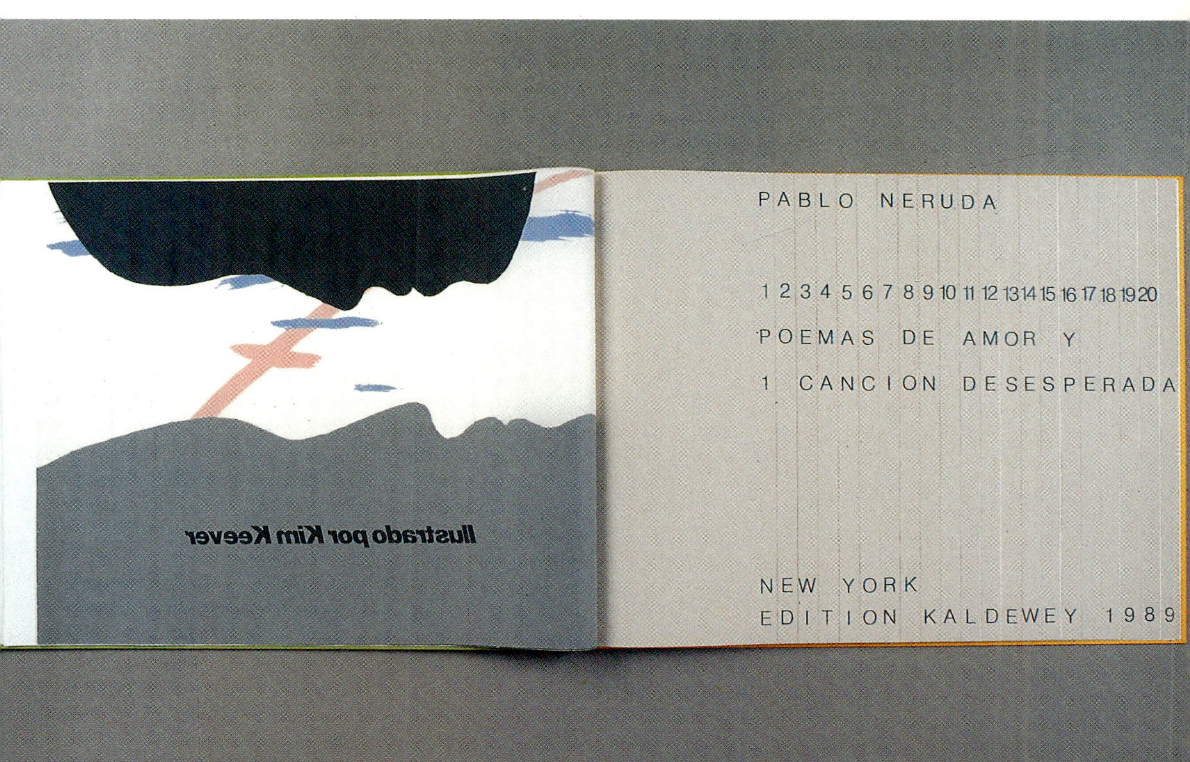

15

Pablo Neruda,
20 poemas de amour.
Title page with illustration by
Kim Keever.

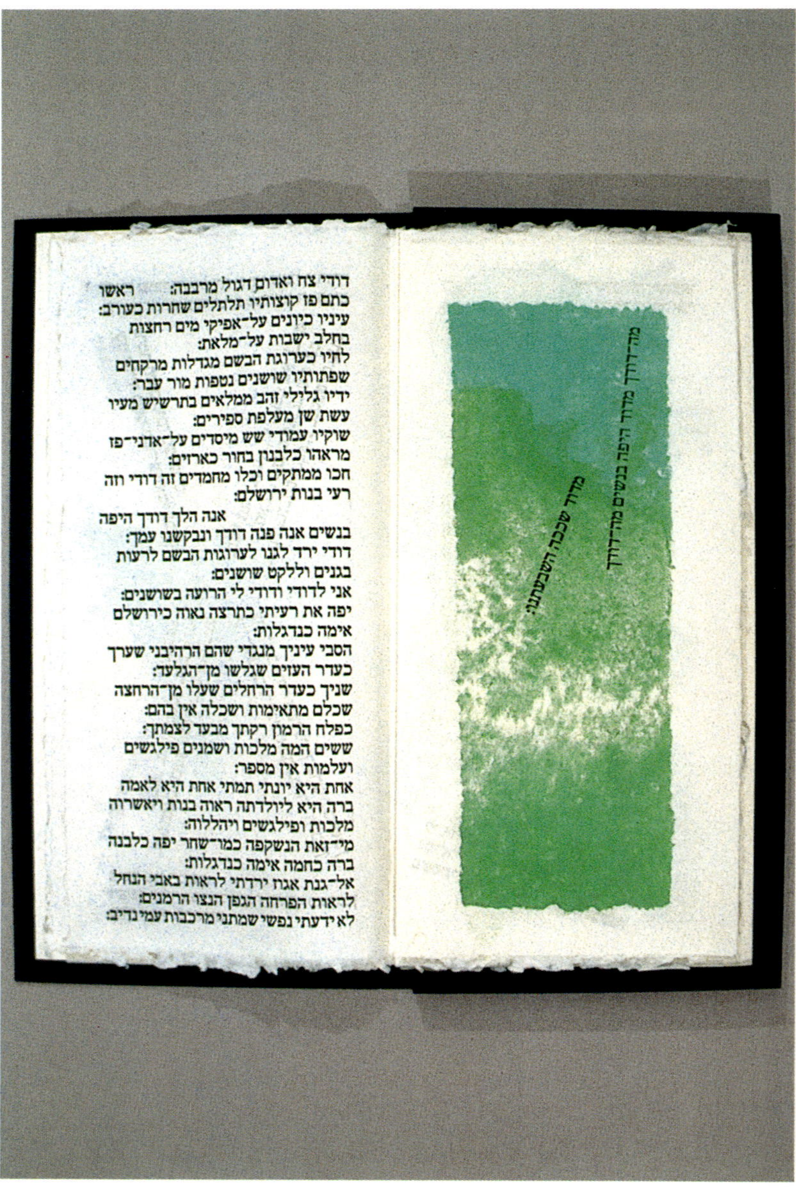

16

Šir Haširim le Šelomo,

Song of Songs.

Paper pulp images.

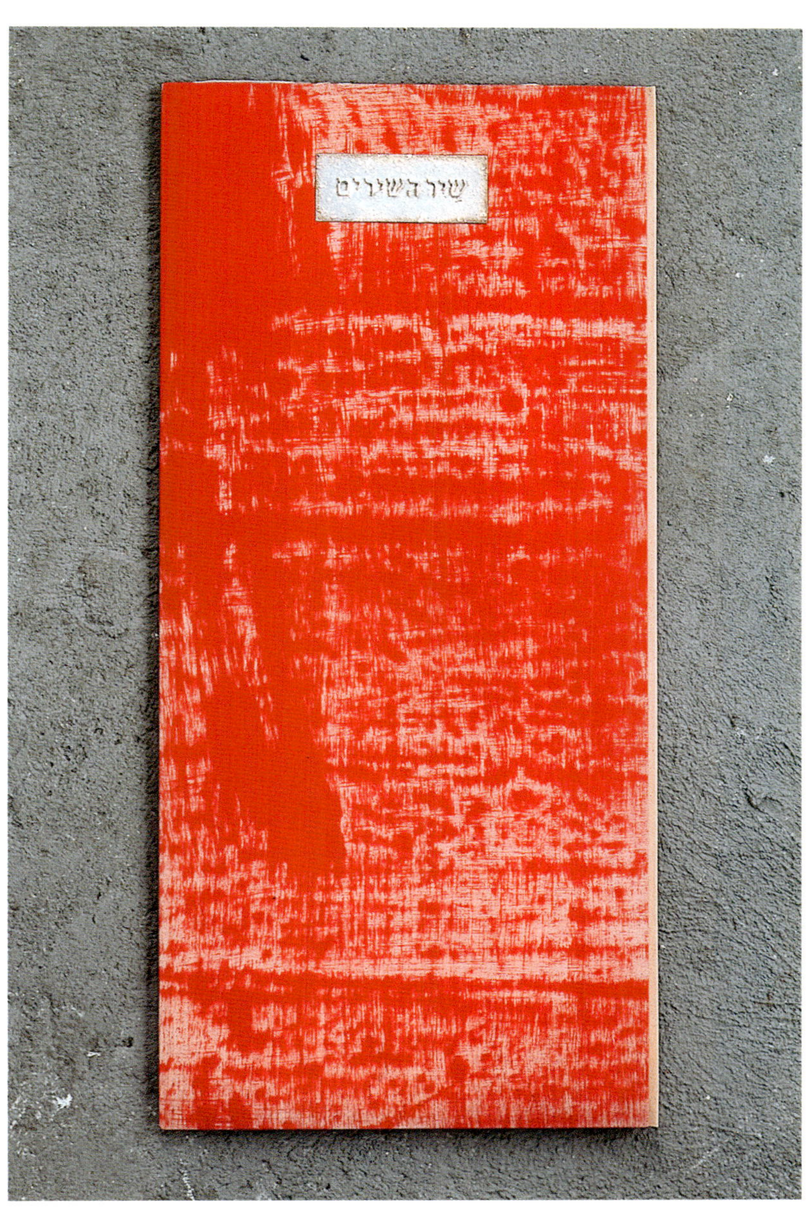

Šir Haširim le Šelomo,
Song of Songs.
Painted calf leather with silver
label.

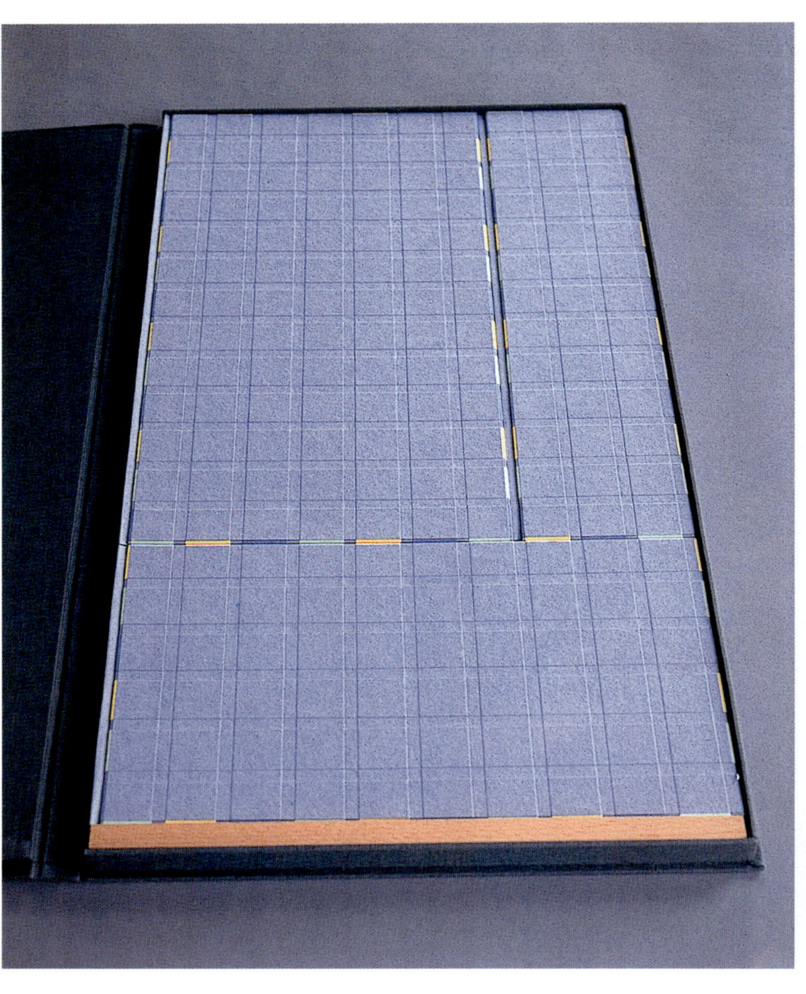

19

Ovid, **Metamorphosis.**
A book in three parts.

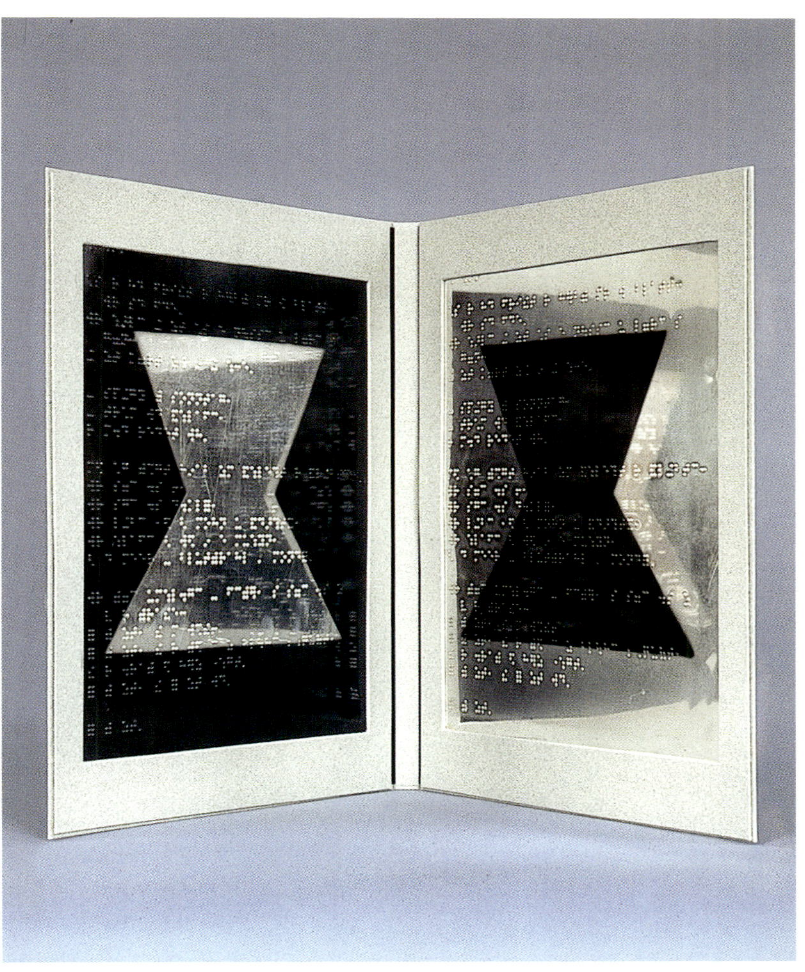

22

Paul Celan,
Sand aus den Urnen.
Braille object by Mischa Kuball.

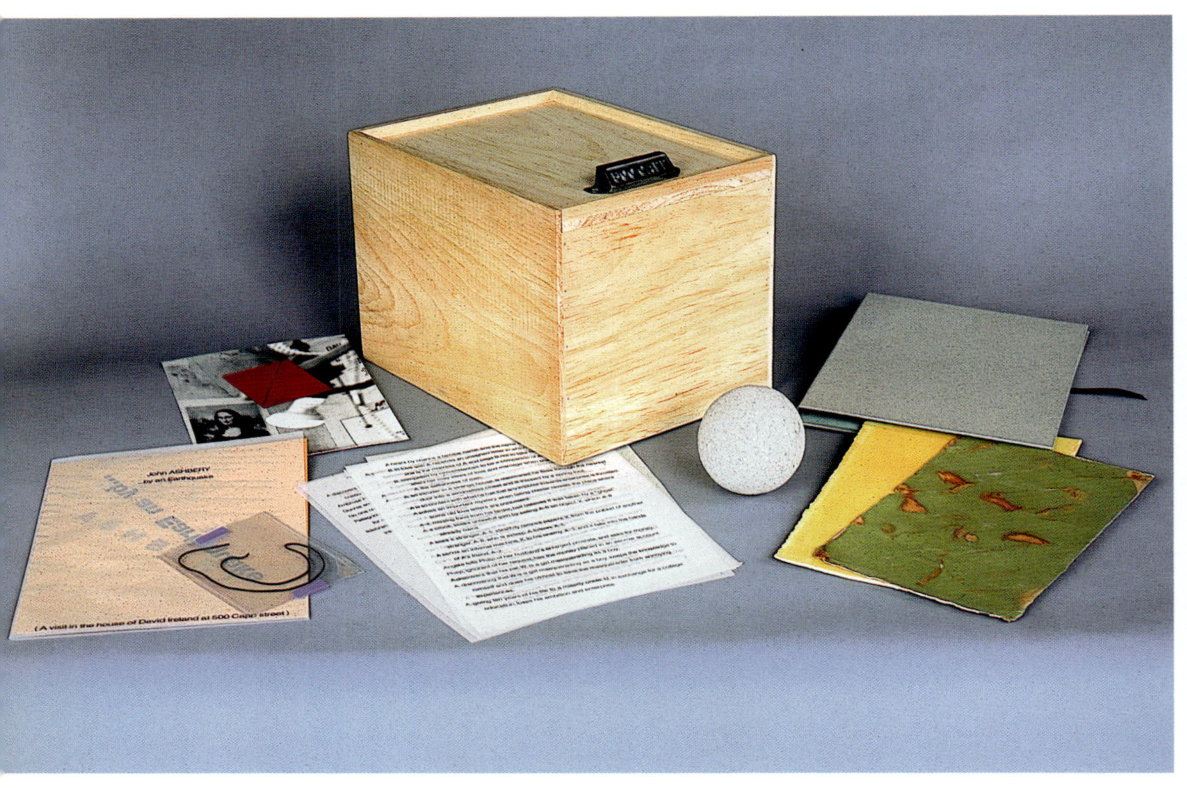

23

John Ashbery,
By an Earthquake.
Objects by David Ireland.

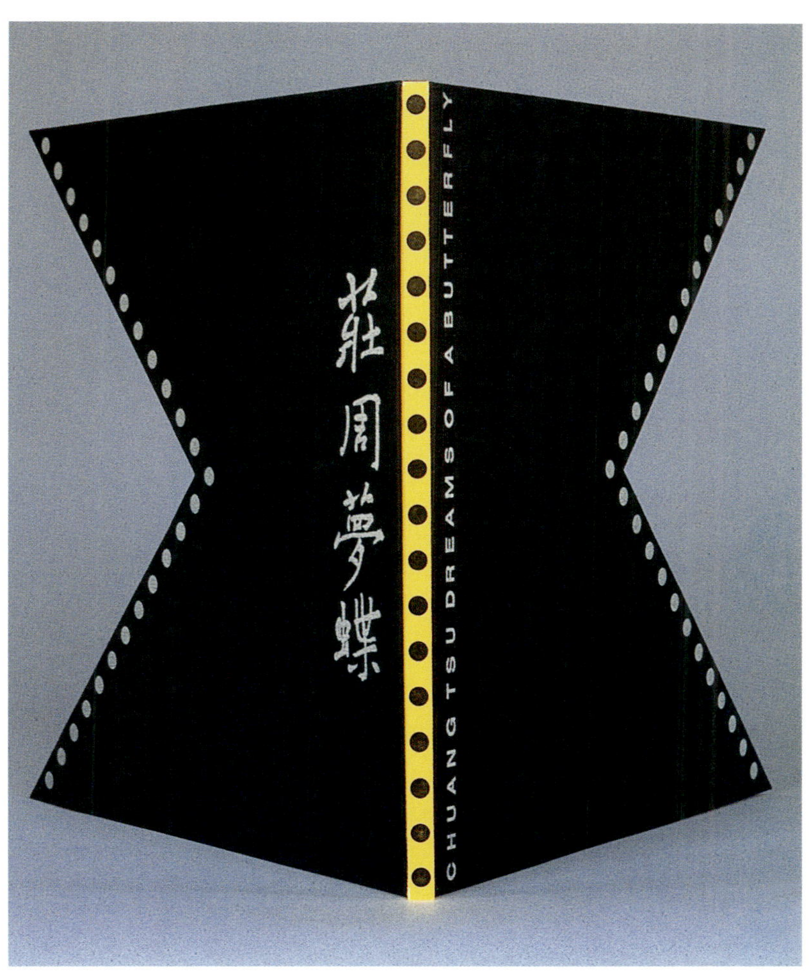

24

Chuang Tsu,
Dream of a Butterfly.
Binding.

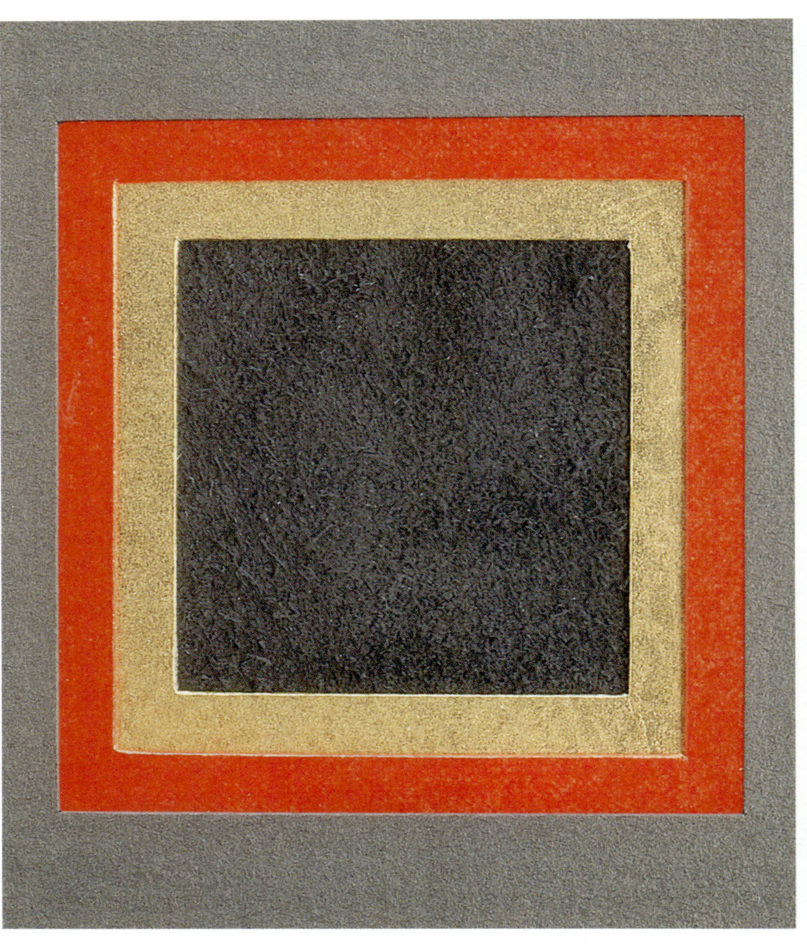

25

The Gyres.
(Source of Imagery.)
Center piece for the front
cover by Richard Tuttle.

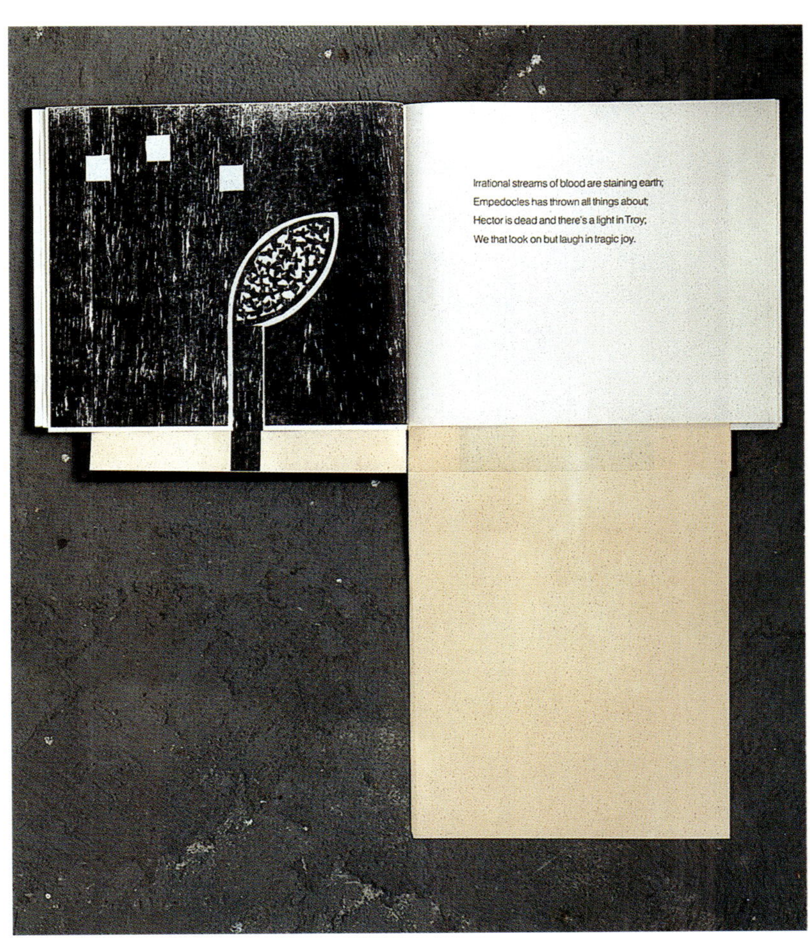

The Gyres.

(Source of Imagery.)

Wood cut by Richard Tuttle.

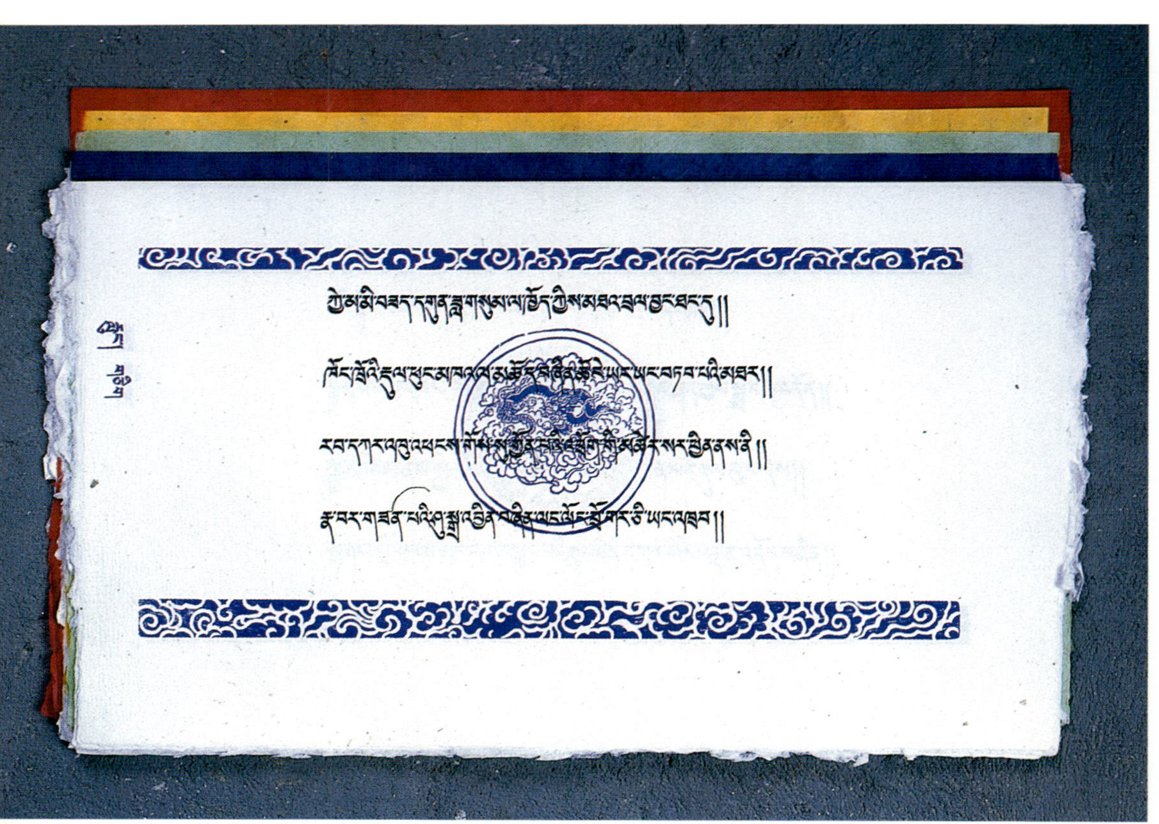

26

The Wind.

Tibetan book by Lha Gyal Tsering.

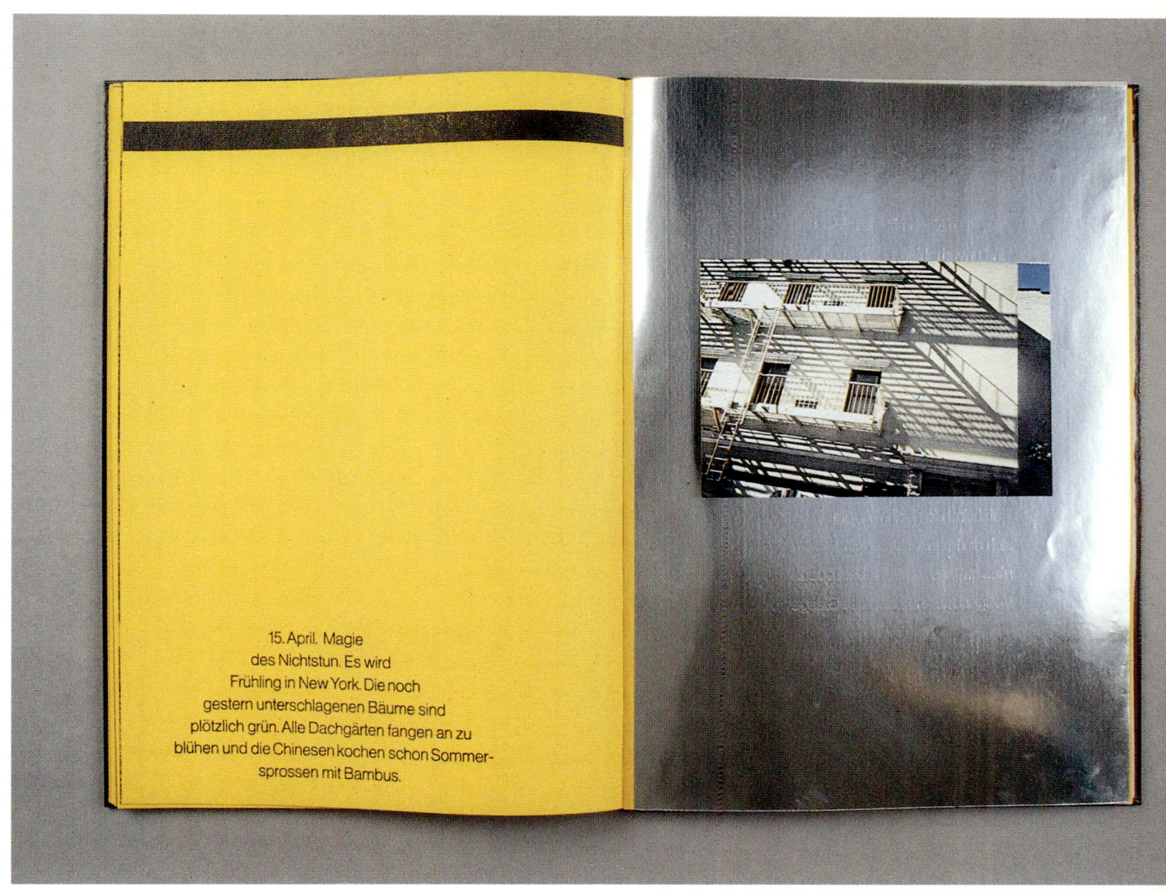

1

New York 1977.

Pages on aluminum paper and
colour xerox.

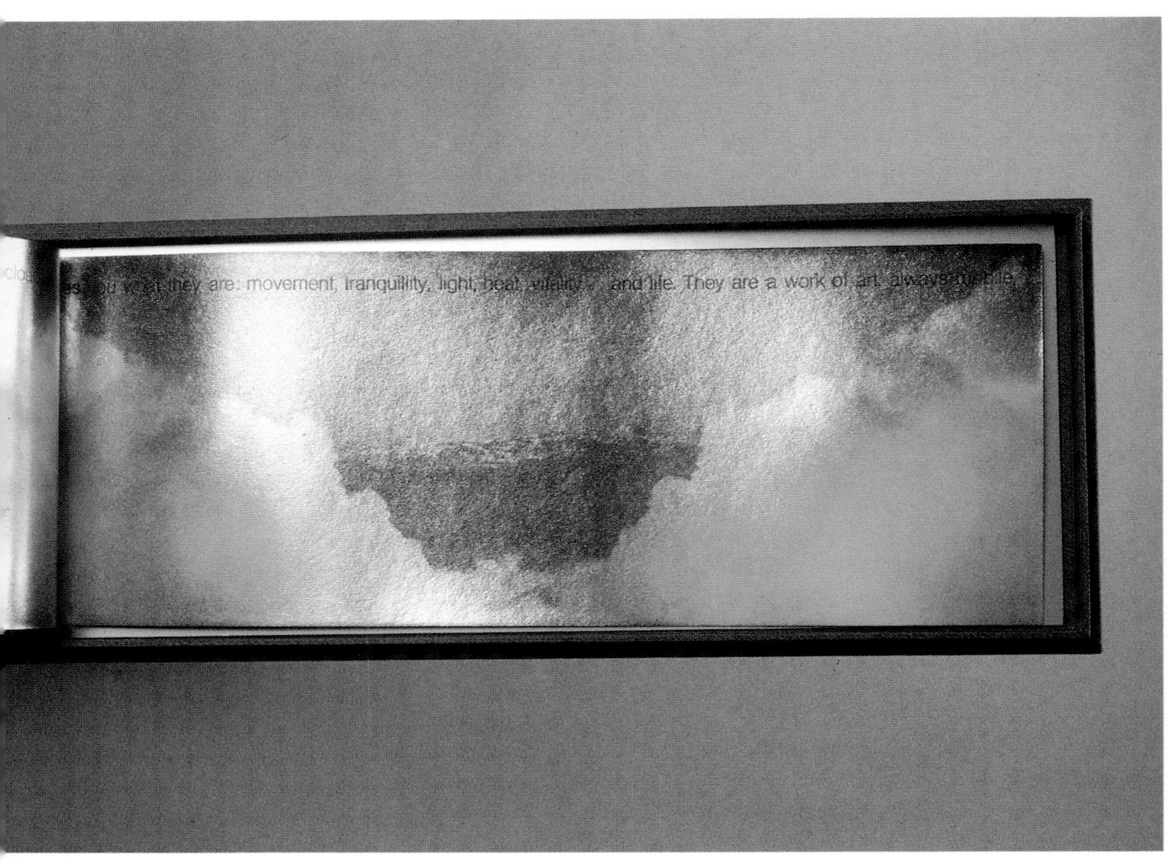

2

Clouds · Wolken

Printed on aluminum.

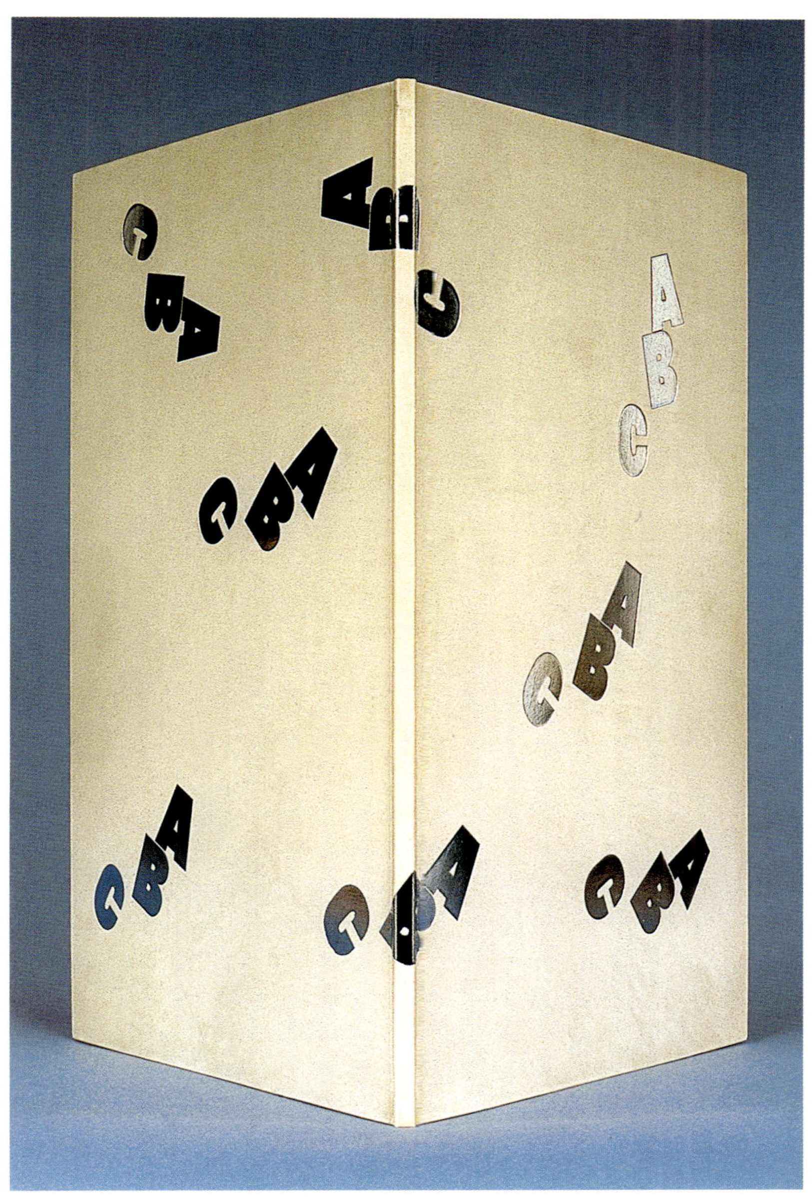

3

ABC.
Calf leather binding by
Christian Zwang.

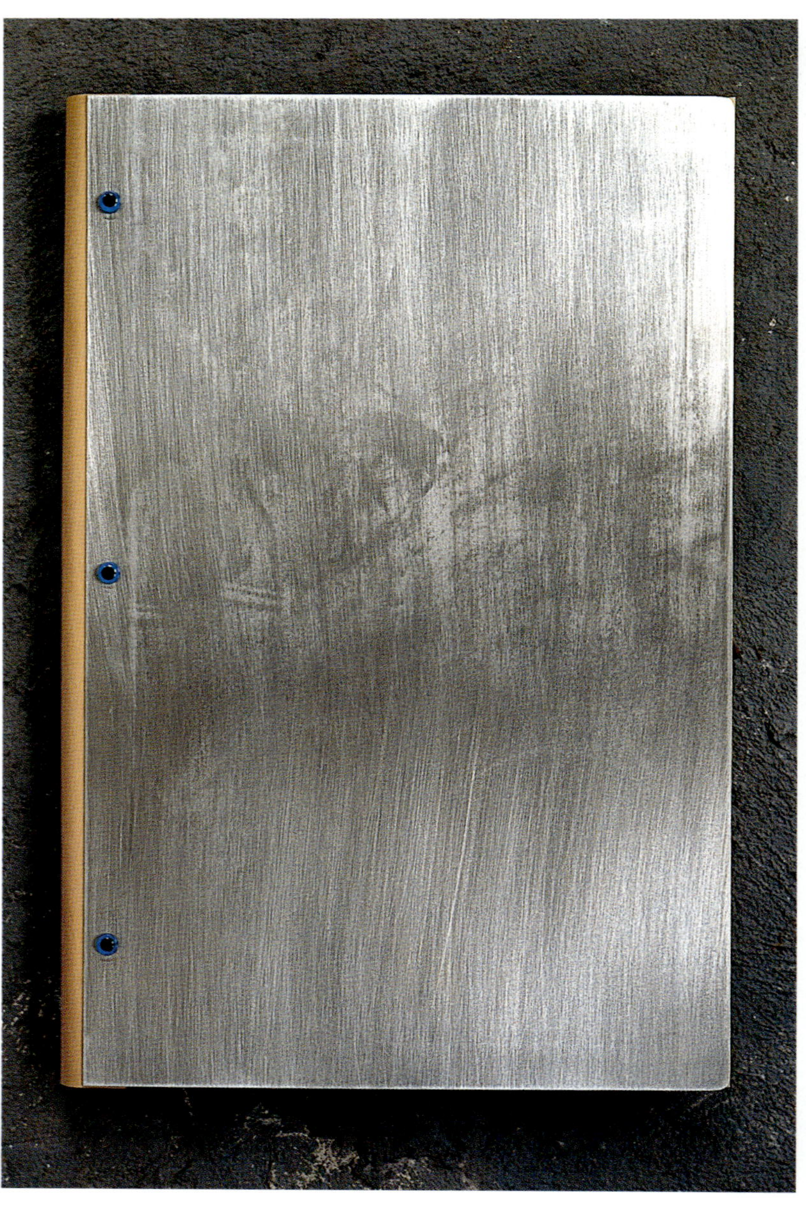

4

Images.
Aluminum binding.

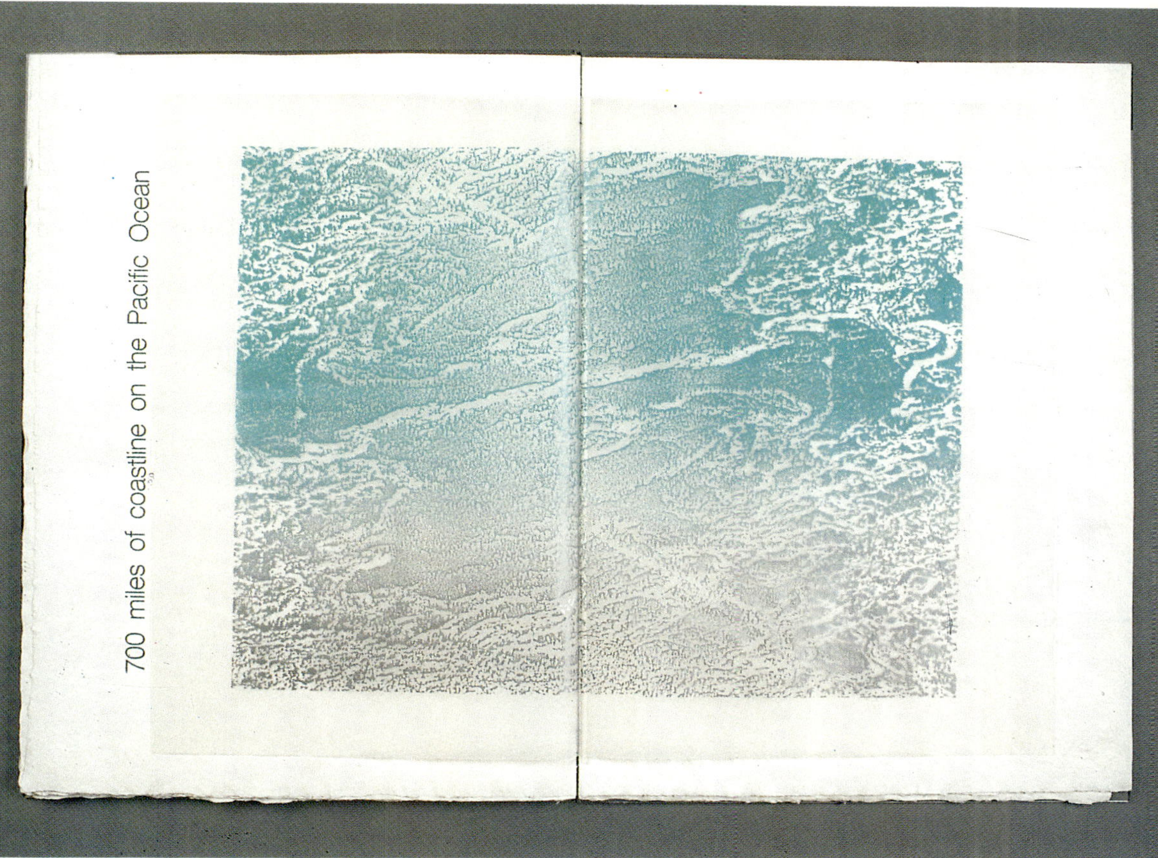

700 miles of coastline on the Pacific Ocean

5

California Time.

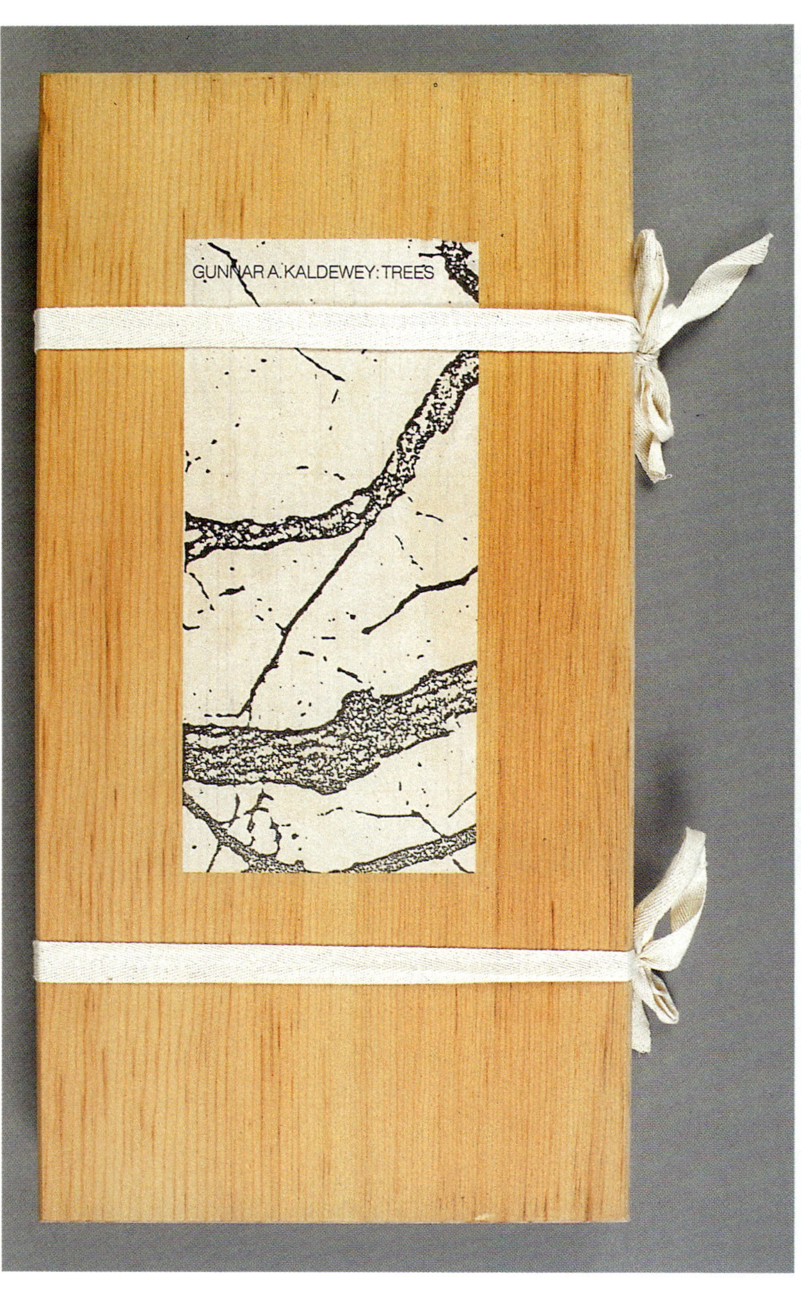

6

Trees.

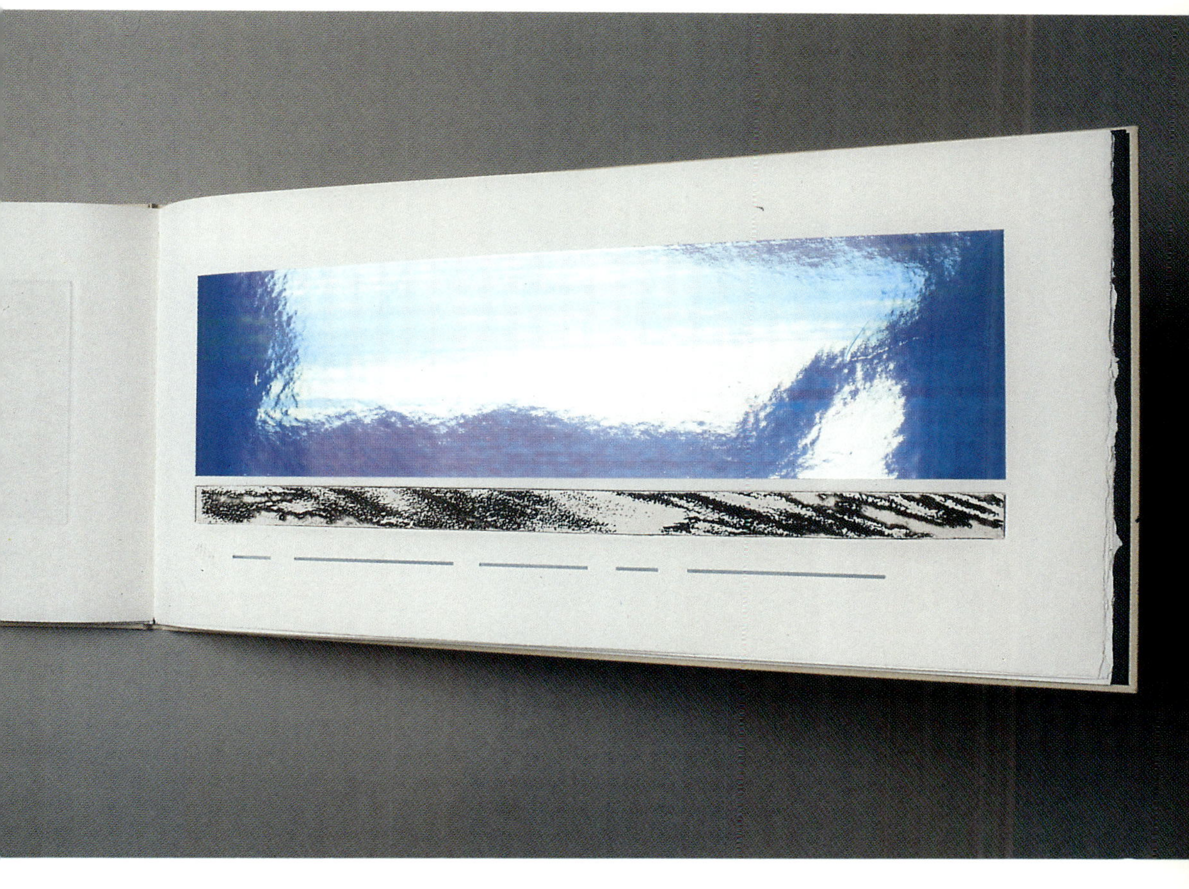

7

Desert.
Etching and fluresent plastic
foil.

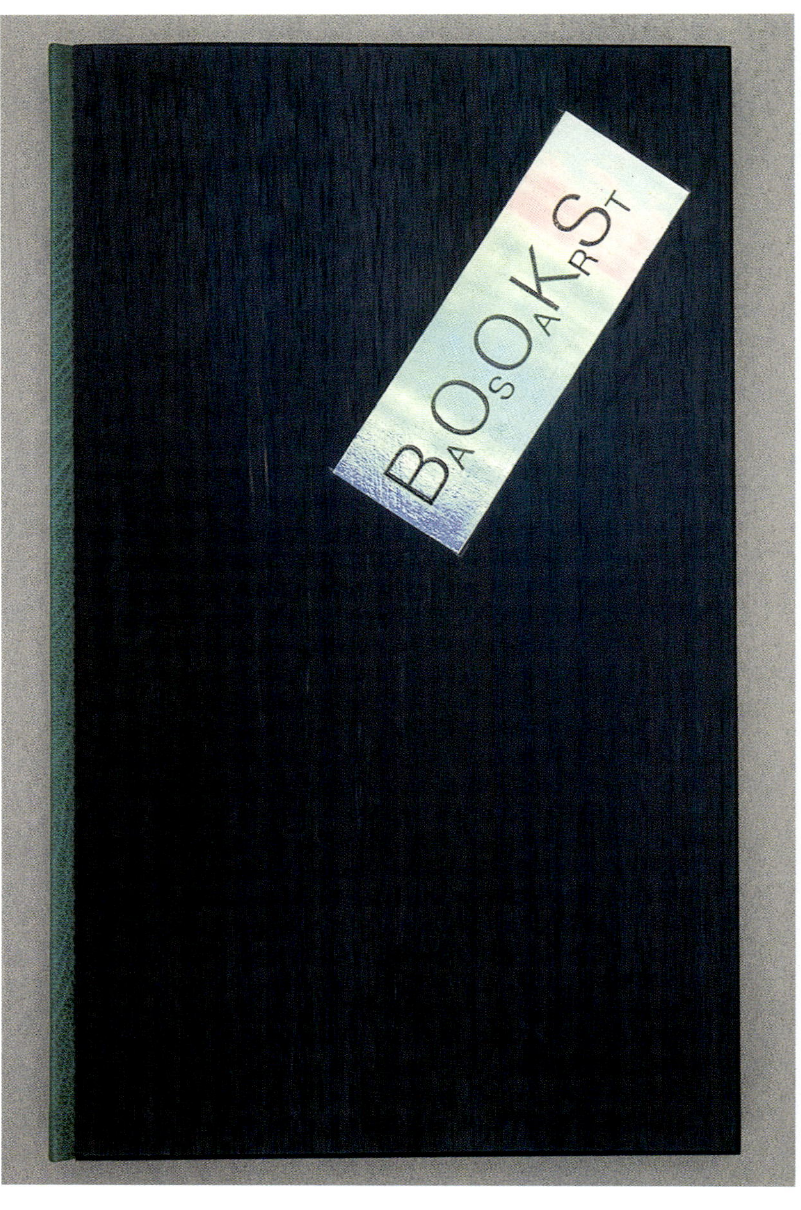

8

Books as Art.
Ebony binding.

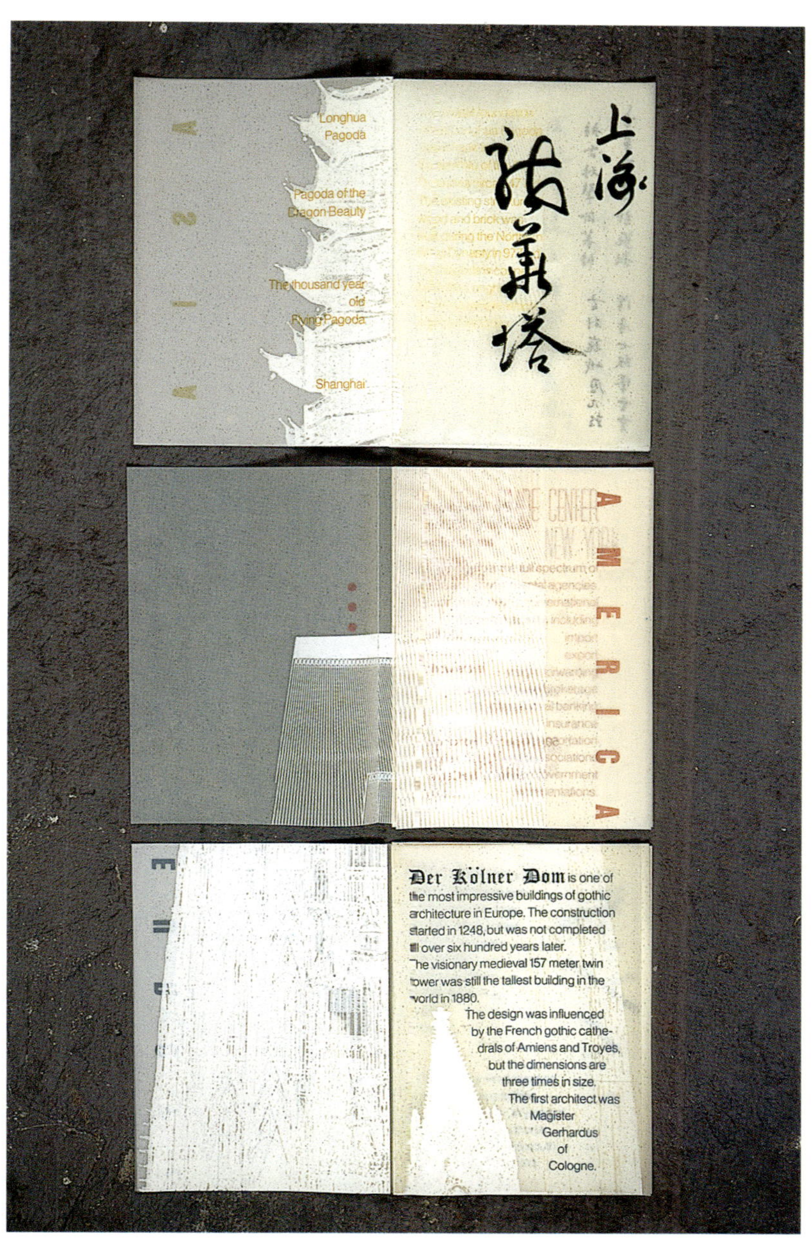

11

Asia · America · Europe.

12

Light Years.
Calf leather binding
by Thomas Zwang.

Double-spread collage.

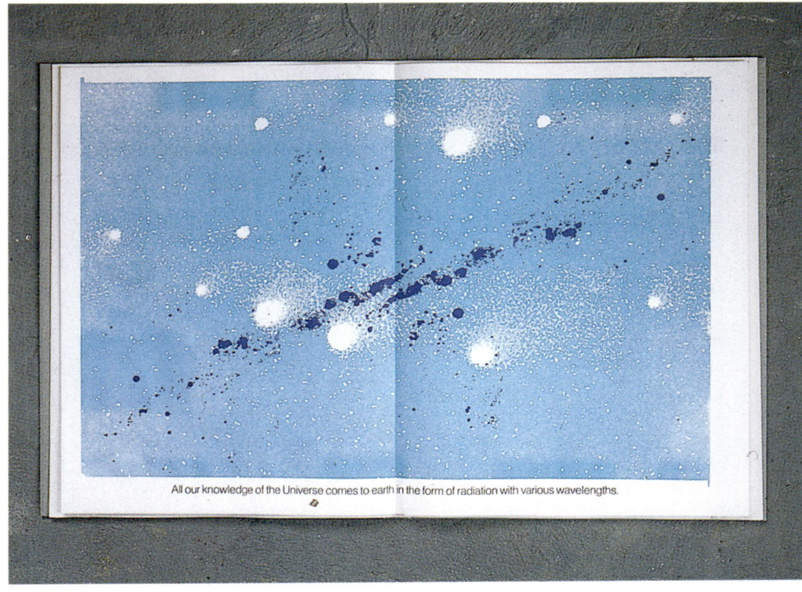

Bibliography / The Books of the Kaldewey Press

The Kaldewey Press was founded in New York in 1985. Books prior to that date were published privately by Gunnar A. Kaldewey in Germany.
The Press issues its books in two groups: ① works done in collaboration with authors and artists and printed by Gunnar A. Kaldewey which appear with the imprint EDITION KALDEWEY, ② works written, illustrated and printed by Gunnar A. Kaldewey himself, with the imprint of KALDEWEY PRESS.

EDITION KALDEWEY 1

Christoph Wecker, New York Reflections Düsseldorf/New York 1980.
Portfolio with 9 color photographs. 44 by 37 cm. In a black clothbox silver lettering.
First Edition. 20 copies. Each photograph signed by the artist. – The images are architectural and of shop window display models in Midtown Manhattan.

EDITION KALDEWEY 2

Everett Potter, Cave Pictures. Düsseldorf/New York 1981. With 3 original pencil drawings by **Jonathan Lasker**. 18 pages, printed in red on Japanese paper. 39 by 20 cm. Black paperboards with inlaid printed label, by C. Zwang.
First Edition. Printed in 25 copies, signed by the author and the artist. The original drawings illustrating the volume vary slightly in each copy.

EDITION KALDEWEY 3

John Eric Broaddus, Sphinx and the Bird of Paradise. Düsseldorf/New York 1981. Title, 14 leaves of cutouts and color Xeroxes, mounted on different paper. 4 pages extensively handcolored by the artist. 31 by 20 cm. In a box.
First edition. John Eric Broaddus (1943 Detroit – 1990 New York) died before finishing this book, the only edition work he did in his life. In 1991, 20 copies were bound in paperboard. In these copies the last three pages are not cut out.
5 deluxe copies, completed by the artist, were bound in turquoise leather by Craig Jensen of Austin, Texas. These copies include an extra suite of nine proof pages, some handcolored by the artist.

EDITION KALDEWEY 4

Kim Keever, Yes and No. Düsseldorf/New York 1982. With 5 woodcuts by Kim Keever, each in several colors. 22 pages. 37 by 28 cm.
First edition. Each woodcut signed by the artist.
30 copies printed on "Scheufelen" paper. Black paperboard with woodcut

label, by Christian Zwang.
5 deluxe copies on Imperial Japanese paper, bound in grey calf gilt and in
black silk box, by C. Zwang.

EDITION KALDEWEY 5

William Burroughs, Mummies. Düsseldorf/New York 1982. With 5 etchings
by **Carl Apfelschnitt**. 30 pages. 37 by 28 cm.
First edition. Each etching is signed by the artist.
70 copies printed on "Scheufelen" paper. Black paperboards with etched
label, by C. Zwang.
5 deluxe copies printed in gold on black Japanese paper, with the etchings
printed in red. Pink calf leather, gilt in black box, by C. Zwang.

EDITION KALDEWEY 6

Christoph Wecker, New York Reflections Two. New York/Düsseldorf 1983.
Portfolio with 10 color photographs. 44 by 37 cm. In a black clothbox, let-
tered in silver.
First edition. 35 copies, each photograph signed by the artist. (Not realized.)

EDITION KALDEWEY 7

Jun Suzuki, In the beginning … New York/Düsseldorf 1984. 12 metal sheets,
each with a Japanese character in red silkscreen print and the English equivalent in cut-out letters underneath; 1 page in letterpress and original brushwork on Japanese paper, mounted on a metal sheet. 30 by 30 cm. Grey paper
box with printed silkscreen labels.
First edition. 35 copies, signed by the artist. The book illustrates the process
of the creation of language. On the last page the first sentence of the earliest
known work of Japanese literature.

EDITION KALDEWEY 8

Wladimir Majakowski, Zakovannaja fil'mos (The celluloid heart). New York
1984. With 10 color xeroxes of the original negative film. Printed in black and
red on brown paper, made by Richard de Bas. Wrappers illustrated with color
xerox, and letterpress title in Russian and English; enclosed in an original circular aluminum film can, also comprising a three meter length of film print
from the original movie. 40 cm in diameter.
First edition. This is the story of Majakowski's motion picture of 1918,
destroyed by fire in the 1930's, as recollected by his lifelong companion Lila
Brik; she discovered the only surviving portion of the film in an old chest during the 1950's, which we acquired from her, together with her reconstruction

of the story, as she remembered it. The surviving strips shows her and Majakowski, the principal actors. – Text in Russian and English. 70 copies.
10 special copies, with additional letterpress text by Vladimir Katanjan, Lila
Brik's companion after Majakowski's death, one original negative of enlarged
stills from the movie made in 1918. Bound in gilt red levant morocco.
4 copies on English de Wint paper for the printer.

EDITION KALDEWEY 9

Paul Celan, Todesfuge. New York 1984. With 6 papercuts by **Mischa Kuball**.
54 pages, printed on transparent and on Fabriano paper. 37 by 28 cm.
First illustrated edition. Signed by the artist.
50 copies bound in black paperboards with printed label, by C. Zwang.
15 special copies bound in flexible vellum gilt, by C. Zwang.
5 deluxe copies (32 by 25 cm) on heavy Japanese paper made for the Kaldewey Press by Shusaku Tomi, Wajima, with 2 original drawings and one
mounted collage by Mischa Kuball, all signed. Loose sheets laid into a
morocco box.

EDITION KALDEWEY 10

Marguerite Duras, Hiroshima mon amour. Synopsis. New York 1985–86.
With 20 paper pulp images by **Ann Sperry**. 32 pages on pink paper, handmade at the Kaldewey mill. 48 by 31 cm.
First illustrated edition. Signed by the artist.
50 copies in loose sheets. Some copies in a grey box lettered in gold by Atelier
Dermont-Duval, Paris. Some copies in a black box lettered in gold by Nello
Nanni, New York.
10 deluxe copies with an extra suite of 5 artist proof sheets made in Aspen
1985, all signed by Ann Sperry. Bound in flexible grey leather with wooden
boards and inlaid metal sheet by Jean de Gonet. In a box.

EDITION KALDEWEY 11

Samuel Beckett, Quatre Poèmes. Four Songs. French and English by Samuel
Beckett. New York 1986. With 6 etchings by **Bun-Ching Lam**. Printed in
green, pink and black on cotton rag paper, made at the Kaldewey mill with
the watermark of the Press. 28 pages in triangular shape. 39 by 40 cm. With
a 45 rpm record of the poems set to music by Bun-Ching Lam.
First book edition.
50 copies bound by C. Zwang in grey paperboards with relief printed covers.
In a rectangular box, spine lettered in silver. Of this regular edition only 40
copies were finally made.
10 special copies on heavy paper with an extra suite of the etchings, printed
in red on Chinese paper. Bound in leather with relief printed covers.

10 deluxe copies an heavy paper with an extra suite of the etchings, printed in red on Chinese paper. Signed by Samuel Beckett and Bun-Ching Lam. Bound in a flexible wooden binding with leather spine and ebony wood corners by Jean de Gonet. The wooden panels on the front cover are in green, on the back in red. In a slip case by Atelier Dermont-Duval, Paris.

EDITION KALDEWEY 12

Pier Paolo Pasolini, Ciant da li ciampanis. **Luisa Famos**, di d'invern. **Andri Peer**, stradun. Poesias rumantschas cun disegns da Not Vital. New York 1987. With five original drawings and one object by **Not Vital**. Printed on paper made from cedar tree bark by Shusaku Tomi in Wajima, Japan. 20 loose pages in flexible wrappers of de Wint paper with a printed label. In a wooden slip case by cabinet maker Shahin, Albany.
First illustrated edition. Signed by the artist.
25 copies on light brown paper. 25 copies on dark brown paper.
10 deluxe copies in an elephant folio format of 100 by 64 cm. Title and colophon handwritten by Not Vital. Printed text on thin paper mounted on the sheets. Bound in wooden cover of Russian birch with two hinges designed by Not Vital and cast in bronze at Pietrasanta, Italy.

EDITION KALDEWEY 13

John Ashbery, Not a First. New York 1987. With three original pencil drawings by **Jonathan Lasker**. 18 pages, printed in blue on cotton rag paper, made at the Kaldewey mill with the watermark of the Press. 30 by 45 cm.
First edition. Signed by the author and the artist.
45 copies in black paperboards, with relief prints after a design by Jonathan Lasker on the front and back cover. Spine lettered in silver by C. Zwang.
10 special copies on large paper. All drawings initialed by the artist. Bound in grey calf leather, with relief prints after a design by Jonathan Lasker on the front and back cover. In a black box by C. Zwang.
10 deluxe copies on large paper. All drawings signed by the artist. Bound in paper over board with an original drawing by Jonathan Lasker (in preparation).

EDITION KALDEWEY 14

Arthur A. Cohen, On the Marionette Theater of Heinrich von Kleist. A Fragment. New York 1988. With 2 full page illustrations, printed from walnut wood blocks and 6 woodcut ornaments in the text by **Elaine Lustig Cohen**. 24 pages on French mould made paper. 41 by 32 cm.
First edition. Signed by the artist.
45 copies in black paperboards, by C. Zwang. Front cover in relief print designed by Elaine Lustig Cohen.

15 deluxe copies on Japanese paper with hand coloring by the artist. Bound
in red English morocco with silver relief print by C. Zwang. In a box.

EDITION KALDEWEY 15

Pablo Neruda, 20 poemas de amour y una canción desperada. New York
1989. 106 pages with 25 linoleum cuts – two double page size – in several
colors by **Kim Keever**. 43 by 56 cm.
First edition with these illustrations. Signed by the artist.
50 copies on white rag paper. Bound in green and yellow paperboards with
printed label by C. Zwang.
20 deluxe copies on Chinese paper. Bound in green leather with printed label
by C. Zwang. In a slipcase.

EDITION KALDEWEY 16

Šir Haširim le Šelomo. The song of songs. Printed in Hebrew and English. New
York 1990. 32 pages on handmade paper of the Press with 10 illustrations of
paper pulp images by **Gunnar A. Kaldewey**. 51 by 24 cm.
First edition with these illustrations. Signed by the printer.
35 copies in loose sheets laid in a blue box, spine lettered in gold.
20 deluxe copies in painted calf leather and a label of etched sterling silver by
C. Zwang. In a slipcase, spine lettered in silver.

EDITION KALDEWEY 17

Confucius, The Great Learning. With an English translation by **Ezra Pound**.
New York 1990–91. 32 pages on handmade paper of the Press with a watermark after a drawing by Not Vital. Chinese calligraphy by **Bun-Ching Lam**.
With 2 drawings and a pencil line drawing by **Not Vital**. 1 sheet on Japanese
paper, coated with silver foil. 81 by 24 cm.
First edition with this illustration. Signed by the artist and the calligrapher.
Chinese seal of the printer.
30 copies in black paperboard with printed silver label by C. Zwang.
10 deluxe copies in loose sheets, laid in two covers of sticks and woven twigs
by Not Vital. In a grey archive box.

EDITION KALDEWEY 18

Franz Kafka, Der Prozess geschrieben von **Hans Peter Willberg**. New York
1990. 58 by 41 cm. 64 pages in silkscreen, 1 page impressum.
First edition of this calligraphic version of Kafka's Trial, written by Hans Peter
Willberg. Signed by Willberg. The silkscreen was executed by Atelier Limited,
Münster.

50 copies in white flexible paperboard with printed label by C. Zwang.
10 deluxe copies in flexible vellum by C. Zwang with a one page original calligraphic manuscript by Hans Peter Willberg. In a slipcase.

EDITION KALDEWEY 19

Ovid, Metamorphosibus Historia Apollinis et Daphnes. Printed in Latin with an English version by **Mary Caponegro**. New York 1992. 3 volumes with 27 illustrations in three colors by **Gunnar A. Kaldewey**. In a grey linen box, spine lettered in silver. 45 by 25 cm.
First edition. Signed by the author and the printer.
45 copies in paperboard with half relief by Cornelia Ahnert of Chemnitz.
12 deluxe copies with an extra suite of the illustrations on Chinese paper, each signed. Bound in flexible leather and in one volume by Cornelia Ahnert.

EDITION KALDEWEY 20

Walter Benjamin, Angelus Novus. Über den Begriff der Geschichte. New York 1993. 49 by 38 cm. 28 pages on rag paper with a watermark of the artist, made at the Kaldewey Press. With 26 full-page woodcuts in several colors by **Heribert Ottersbach**.
First illustrated edition. 50 copies in paperboard with wood cut label.
10 deluxe copies on Chinese paper. In a flexible calf leather binding with five grommets, executed by Cornelia Ahnert.
All copies are signed by Heribert Ottersbach.

EDITION KALDEWEY 21

Seamus Heaney and James Joyce, Sandymount Strand. New York 1993. 44 by 36 cm in circular shape. 28 pages on rag paper with a watermark of the artist, made at the Kaldewey Press. With 12 etchings in two colors by **Felim Egan**.
First edition. 40 copies in loose sheets in a box by Judy Conant.
12 deluxe copies handcolored by the artist. Bound in green calf leather with an inlaid aluminum label by Christian Zwang.
All copies are signed by Seamus Heaney and Felim Egan.

EDITION KALDEWEY 22

Paul Celan, Der Sand aus den Urnen. New York 1994. 38 by 28 cm. 66 pages in braille and letterpress. With 15 original acryl drawings by **Mischa Kuball**.
50 copies in paperboard with printed label by Craig Jensen of Austin, Texas.
15 deluxe copies in grey calf leather blind stamped by Cornelia Ahnert. In a slipcase with two metal objects, painted by Mischa Kuball.

This is the second volume of the Kaldewey edition of Celan's "Mohn und Gedächtnis", illustrated by Mischa Kuball.
All copies are signed by Mischa Kuball.

EDITION KALDEWEY 23

John Ashbery, ... by an Earthquake. (A visit in the house of David Ireland at 500 Capp street.) New York 1994. Multiple in a wooden box 32 by 24 by 22 cm. 6 pages poem by John Ashbery, also printed in two posters, one signed by Ashbery. With 6 original objects by **David Ireland** and several photos and kodaliths of the work of Mr. Ireland by Abe Frajndlich.
First edition. Multiple box in 46 copies.
David Ireland transformed his house at 500 Capp street in San Francisco in a "Gesamtkunstwerk" and the multiple with its three layers of folders reflects this house.
The wooden boxes are made by Shahin cabinet maker in Albany.
The handle of the box was specially cast for the edition.
2 copies of the signed poster for John Ashbery and Gunnar A. Kaldewey were printed on handmade rag paper.

EDITION KALDEWEY 24

Chuang Tsu dreams of a butterfly. Translated from the ancient Chinese and calligraphy by **Bun-Ching Lam**. Chinese and English.
New York 1995. 31 by 31 cm in sculptural shape. With 8 handcolored etchings by **Gunnar A. Kaldewey**. 40 pages on old Chinese paper. Black paperboard with a yellow spine by Thomas Zwang. In a slipcase.
First edition with these illustrations. Printed in 40 copies. Signed and with the Chinese Seal of the printer.

EDITION KALDEWEY 25

W. B. Yeats, The Gyres. (Source of Imagery.) New York 1995. 38 by 38 cm. With 6 wood cuts and one metal cut by **Richard Tuttle**, printed in grey, black, silver and gold. 56 pages, folded into each other.
First illustrated edition. 50 copies an yellow and white paper, made at the Kaldewey Press with the watermark of the artist. Bound in black paperboard by Thomas Zwang. In a slipcase.
10 deluxe copies on Chinese paper, bound in back calf leather by Thomas Zwang. Front cover with a golden and red inlaid doublure by Richard Tuttle. In a slipcase.
The wood blocks are cut and printed by Richard Tuttle.
All copies are signed by the artist.

EDITION KALDEWEY 26

Lha Gyal Tsering, The Wind. A Tibetan poem with an English translation by Pema Bhum. New York 1996. 52 loose pages with 20 wood cuts by **Lobsang Wangchu** and each page with two wood cut borders. Printed in four colors on handmade cotton rag paper of the Kaldewey Press. 27:51 cm. Insert with colored Tibetan paper and housed in two black relief card boards, made by Tibetan Handicraft Paper Industry.
First illustrated edition. 45 copies in a grey slipcase by Judi Conant, Vermont. 10 deluxe copies in magnolia wood covers, carved at the workshop of Migmargyalpo Lama in Kathmandu. In a red and gold silk chemise laid in a box.

KALDEWEY PRESS 0

Franz Blei, Grimod de la Renière. Hamburg 1976.
With 1 illustration. 16 pages on old yellow Imperial Japanese paper.
28 by 17 cm. Black paperboards, on front cover illustration originally designed by Grimod, executed in relief print. Black box lined aluminum foil, by C. Zwang.
The first book printed by Gunnar Kaldewey in 1976 for his gourmet friends. 30 copies, a few on simple white paper.

KALDEWEY PRESS 1

New York 1977. Hamburg 1978.
60 pages on different paper and on plastic, with 23 color xeroxes.
51 by 37 cm. Black boards, with original New York subway token mounted on the front cover, in box covered with silver plastic material, in center circular opening revealing the subway token on the binding, fluorescent plastic spine, by C. Zwang.
First edition. Text in German, English and French. Signed by the author-printer.
42 copies on white Fabriano paper.
8 special copies, printed on Fabriano paper, specially tinted yellow by offset process, binding as above.

KALDEWEY PRESS 2

Clouds · Wolken. Düsseldorf/New York 1982.
26 pages on aluminum sheets. Printed in blue letterpress on a black offset background, each page individually sprayed in various colors suggesting cloud formations. 10 by 45 cm. Polished aluminum covers with hinges of stainless steel. – In a grey linen box lettered in silver, by C. Zwang.

First edition. Signed by the author-printer.
30 copies in English.
30 copies in German.

KALDEWEY PRESS 3

ABC. New York/Düsseldorf 1983.
Frontispiece on plastic sheet with silkscreen print. 29 pages on onion skin
paper made by Edgeworth, USA. Printed in blue and purple. Endleaves of silver paper decorated with car spray in three colors. 46 by 29 cm.
First edition. Signed by the printer.
20 copies on green paper. Flexible covers of silver plastic with silkscreen
image. Grey box, spine lettered in silver, by C. Zwang.
15 special copies on green, blue and yellow paper in grey calf, richly silvered,
by C. Zwang. In a grey box.
7 deluxe copies on rose onion skin paper; binding of calf leather specially
dyed in England to match the color of the paper, richly gilt, by C. Zwang.
Black silk box.

KALDEWEY PRESS 4

Images · New York 1986. 20 pages with paper pulp images in red and blue
by Gunnar Kaldewey, on loft-dried cotton rag paper. 45 by 29 cm. Aluminum
cover with a leather spine. In a box lettered in silver.
First edition. The first book with paper by Cunnar Kaldewey, handmade in
Aspen, Colorado 1985 under the supervision of Margaret Prentice (founder
of Twinrocker Paper). Seven copies were made. Signed by the author-printer.
The book was delivered to the subscribers in 1992.

KALDEWEY PRESS 5

California Time · New York 1987. 36 pages on English handmade paper
with 16 illustrations in linecut-monoprints. Letterpress printing in several colors. 51 by 38 cm.
First edition. Signed by the author-printer.
45 copies in a Plexiglass binding by C. Zwang. Orange box lettered in silver.
7 special copies on heavy Fabriano paper. Loose sheets in a vellum cover;
placed in an orange box.
15 deluxe copies with an extra suite of the illustrations on transparent paper,
62 by 42 cm. All signed. Bound in turquoise leather with an inlaid pink label
by C. Zwang. In a box lettered in silver.

KALDEWEY PRESS 6

Trees · New York 1988. 42 folded pages on 7 sheets. 49 by 61 cm.
With 17 linecut-monoprint illustrations on hand-colored backgrounds
by Gunnar Kaldewey. 30 point Futura letterpress on Japanese paper, made
by Shusaku Tomi in Wajima, Japan for the Press.
First Edition. Signed by the author-printer.
40 copies on heavy brown paper, bound with spines of Brazilian rosewood.
In a wooden box with two strings and printed label.
18 deluxe copies on light brown paper and unfolded. With an extra suite of
the illustrations on Papier de Chine. Bound in old Dutch Chagrin-paper with
two large illustrations on the front cover, embossed in leather by C. Zwang.
Spine lettered in silver. In a box, lettered in silver.
3 copies for the printer, bound in calf leather by C. Zwang.

KALDEWEY PRESS 7

The Desert · New York 1989. Suite of 7 etchings with letterpress printing.
With two cassette recording the sounds of the desert during the day and at
night. 19 pages.
First edition. Signed by the author-printer.
5 deluxe copies in Folio on black paper with two additional etchings.
52 by 56 cm. Binding coated with desert sand. In a box.
40 copies in Quarto on white paper. 26 by 56 cm. Bound in paperboard with
relief print by C. Zwang. The paper for both editions was made at the Kaldewey Press.

KALDEWEY PRESS 8

Books as art. **A lecture**. Los Angeles 1990. With 14 etchings in green and
blue. 36 pages on handmade paper of the Kaldewey Press and on fluorescent
plastic sheets. Printed in three colors. 25 by 16 cm. Bound in a binding with
two ebony covers, spine in green morocco. Fluorescent printed plastic label.
In a box by C. Zwang.
First edition. A lecture given by Gunnar A. Kaldewey in 1990 at the Getty
Center, Los Angeles; at the Museum of Fine Arts, Boston; at Galleri Aktuell
Kunst, Oslo; at the Museum of Art, Baltimore and at Harvard University.
Signed by the author-printer.
20 copies on white paper. 20 copies on multicolor paper.

KALDEWEY PRESS 9

Changing waters volume 1: The Hudson River. New York 1991. 10-meter-fold-
out-book. With many illustrations printed in four colors. On handmade paper
of the Press. 12,5 by 65 cm. Light green leather binding with a black spine by

C. Zwang. In a box lettered in silver.
First edition. Signed by the printer.
40 regular copies. The leather was specially made and dyed in New York.
10 hand-colored deluxe copies with an extra suite of the illustrations on Chinese paper.

KALDEWEY PRESS 10

Changing waters volume 2: Der Rhein. New York 1992. 11-meter-fold-out-book. With 7 hand colored plates mountec on white paper and a double page printed with blind stamping. 12,5 by 65 cm. Dark green leather binding with a black spine by C. Zwang. In a box lettered in silver.
First edition. Signed by the printer. The text was printed in Romantsch, Switzerdütsch, French, German, English and Dutch. – Both volumes of "Changing Waters" are dedicated to John Cage.
Both volumes were delivered in a dos à dos box or in separate single boxes.
40 regular copies.
10 deluxe copies with an extra suite of the plates on Chinese paper, handcolored and signed.

KALDEWEY PRESS 11

Asia · America · Europa. New York 1994. 3 scrolls in the size of 100:70 cm. Printed in Chinese, English and German. 3 booklets with 90 pages in several colors, 1 page colophon. In a linen cloth box by Judy Conant. 51 by 24 by 9 cm.
First edition. 40 copies regular edition.
10 handcolored deluxe copies.
Silkscreen by Kicherer, Stuttgart.
All copies are signed by the printer.

KALDEWEY PRESS 12

Light Years.
New York 1996. With eight double-page illustrations by Gunnar A. Kaldewey, printed with metal cuts in several colors. 4C pages on Johannot paper. 44:34 cm.
First edition. Signed by the printer.
45 copies in loose sheets in a slipcase.
7 deluxe copies with an extra suite of the illustrations, signed and numbered by the printer. Bound in calf leather, richly gilt, by Thomas Zwang of Hamburg. Two copies in grey leather and five copies in black leather.

Biography

Born 1946 in Fehmarn, an island between Denmark and Germany.

Founded a rare book company, specializing in French and German literature
of the 18th century, published 75 annotated catalogues. Branches of the
company in Munich, Hamburg, Düsseldorf, Paris and New York 1971–1984.

1985 founded the Kaldewey Press in Poestenkill, New York, publishing
contemporary artist books in collaborating with writers and visual artists.

Lives in New York City and Poestenkill, New York.

Exhibitions / Presentations of the Kaldewey Press (selected)

1996 Köln, Artistbook International
New York, Kisch & Gadella Gallery
Tampa, Graphicstudio, University of Southern Florida

1995 New York, Second Artist book International
Leipzig, Deutsche Bücherei

1994 Bloomington, Indiana, Lilly Library
New York, Ursus Books & Prints
Paris, First Artist Book International

1993 Paris, Galerie Yvon Lambert (catalogue)
New York, John Lee Gallery
Dublin, Museum of Modern Art
Williamstown, Williams College Chapin Library
Minneapolis, Center for Book Arts
Hamburg, Kunsthalle Foyer

1992 New York, Marlborough Gallery (artist book show)
Hannover, Galerie Stula

1991 New York, Grolier Club
Boston, Space Gallery (catalogue)

1990 Cambridge, Harvard University (catalogue)
Baltimore, Museum of Art
Oslo, Galleri Aktuell Kunst
Bennington College, Crossett Library
Boston, Museum of Fine Arts
Los Angeles, Getty Center

1989 New York, Ex Libris
Amsterdam, Picaron Gallery
Santa Barbara, University of California

1988 New York, Metropolitan Museum of Art (catalogue)
Boston, Boston Athenaeum (Traveling show)
New York, Ursus Books and Prints (catalogue)
Hamburg, Felix Jud
San Francisco, Mills College

1987 Los Angeles, Jan Turner Gallery
New York, Center for Book Arts (included in two shows)
Düsseldorf, Galerie Niepel
New York, New York Public Library

1986 New York, Tibor de Nagy Gallery
Frankfurt, Stiftung Buchkunst in Deutsche Bibliothek
Chicago, Cultural Center Goethe House
Hannover, Kunstverein
Boston, Bromer Booksellers

1985 Hamburg, Galerie Zwang

Articles and Reviews

Wye, Deborah, Thinking Print. Books to Billboards, 1980–95. New York, Museum of Modern Art 1996.
(Hirsch, Faye) Tibetian journey. New York, On Paper 1996.
Brody, Jacqueline, Gunnar Kaldewey & Chuang-Tsu. New York, PCN 1996.

Brody, Jacqueline, Richard Tuttle and W. B. Yeats. New York, PCNL 1995.
Seegers, U. (Hrsg.) Holz/Schnitt: Manuell oder maschinell gefertigter Originaldruck. Köln, Gothaer
Kunstforum 1995.
Kahlefendt, N., Babylonisches Sprachgewirr in den Setzkästen. Frankfurt, Börsenblatt 1995.
Brody, Jacqueline, Mischa Kuball & Paul Celan. New York, PCNL 1995.
Castleman, Riva, A century of artist books. Between the pages. New York 1995.

Gambihler, R., Sechs Steine und fünf Tonnen Satz: Kaldeweys bibliophile Drucke in der Deutschen Bücherei.
    Leipzig, Volkszeitung 1994.
Castleman, Riva, A Century of artists books. New York, Museum of Modern Art 1994.
(swi), Mit der Haut erfahren. Mischa Kuballs Buch mit Celan Gedichten. Düsseldorf, Westdeutsche Zeitung
    1994.
Lucius, W. D. v., La Maison des Pages. Frankfurt, Imprimatur 1994.
Brody, Jacqueline, Heribert Ottersbach & Walter Benjamin. New York, PCNL 1994.
Rainwater, R., The American Livre de Peintre. New York, Grolier Club 1994.
Dooley, M., Feeling Free: Bookworks at the Getty. New York, Print 1994.

Cunningham, F., The ultimate stocking filler. The Sandymount Strand book. Dublin, Sunday Business Post
    1993.
Reed, Marcia, Contemporary Artists' Books. Los Angeles, The J. Paul Getty Trust bulletin 1993.
Volz, Robert L. and Wayne G. Hammond, The Kaldewey Press of Poestenkill, New York. Williamstown,
    Chapin Library 1993.
Williams College, Bicentennial convocation. Williamstown 1993.
Antonetti, M., Une conversation avec Gunnar A. Kaldewey à Poestenkill, New York. In catalogue: Livres
de Peintre. Artist Books. Paris, Yvon Lambert 1993.
Bright, Betty, The Kaldewey Press. Minneapolis, Minnesota Center for Book Art 1993.
Woodworth, P., Rising tide for Felim Egan. Dublin, Times 1993.

Lucius, W. D. v., Beispiele der Einbandkunst. Stuttgart, Buchbinder Colleg 1992.
(Ekkart, R.) Een boekmuseum verzamelt. Gravenhage, Meermanno-Westreenianum 1992.
(Ready, Tara), Books and Portfolios. Exhibition catalogue. New York, Marlborough 1992.
Russell, John, »Drawn in the 90's,« New York, New York Times June 28, 1992.
Kirshenbaum, Sandra, Printed responses to the written word. Catalogue.
New York, Cooper Union 1992.
Rainwater, Robert, Signs of Life: Not Vital's prints & books. New York, PCNL 1992.

Schulz, P. O., Schöpfer der Bücher. Hamburg, Ambiente 1991.
Stutzer, Beat, Not Vital Druckgraphik & Multiples. Chur 1991.
McGregor, Stella Aguirre, Artist's books of the 80's & beyond. Boston, Space 1991.

Brody, Jacqueline, The silver page. New York, PCNL 1990.

Hightower, Marvin, The artist's book. Cambridge, Harvard Gazette 1990.

Edelstein, J. M., The book made art. Catalogue. Harvard University 1990.

Anninger, Anne, Introduction to exhibition catalogue. Harvard University 1990.

Brody, Jacqueline, The Kaldewey way. New York, PCNL 1990.

Garvey, Eleanor M., Gunnar Kaldewey of den postmoderne bok (translated by Erik Aarsland). Oslo, Galleri Aktuell Kunst 1990.

Huther, Christian, Art Frankfurt. München, Weltkunst 1990.

von Lucius, Wulf D., Künstlerbücher auf der Messe. Frankfurt, FAZ 1989.

Alert, Boek & Kunst. Amsterdam, Alert 1989.

Kirshenbaum, Sandra, Artist Books of the Kaldewey Press. San Francisco, Fine Print 1989.

Brody, Jacqueline, The Kaldewey Press at the Metropolitan Museum. New York, Print collector's newsletter 1988.

Coron, Antoine, Books from New Atlantis. New York, Metropolitan Museum 1988.

Garvey, Eleanor, Gunnar Kaldewey and the post-modern book. New York, Metropolitan Museum 1988.

Kraus, Peter and Wyer, William, The Kaldewey Press at Ursus Books. New York, Ursus Books 1988.

Strauss, Monica, Edition Kaldewey. San Francisco, Fine Print 1988.

Wick, Peter A., »Artists of the Book 1988«, catalogue. Boston, Athenaeum 1988.

Spindler, Albert, Bibliographie deutschsprachiger Handpressen seit 1945. Hamburg, Merlin 1988.

Buchausstellung bei Felix Jud. Hamburg, Die Welt 1988.

Lambrecht, Susanne, Vier Gedichte im Ebenholz-Dreieck. Düsseldorf, Rheinische Post 1987.

Düsseldorfer verkauft Literatur in Dosen. Bücherschätze in der Galerie Niepel. Düsseldorf, Express 1987.

American Prints 1960–1985 in the Collection of the Museum of Modern Art, Catalogue raisonné. Ed. by Riva Castleman. New York 1986.

von Helmolt, Christa, Künstlerbücher von höchstem Anspruch. Frankfurt, Frankfurter Allgemeine Zeitung 1986.

»Klein aber fein«. Hannover, Hannoversche Zeitung 1986.

Wertvolle Künstlerbücher in Frankfurt. Heidelberg, Rhein-Neckar Zeitung 1986.

Kaldewey Press bei Stiftung Buchkunst. Saarbrücken, Saarbrücker Zeitung 1986.

Buchkunst in alter Tradition. Berlin, Tagesspiegel 1986.

Stiftung Buchkunst zeigt Künstlerbücher. Mainz, Allgemeine Zeitung 1986.

Kostbarkeiten für Bücherfreunde. Heilbronn, 1986.

Künstlerbücher. Darmstadt, Darmstädter Tagblatt 1986.

Hoffberg, Judith, Kaldewey Press. Los Angeles, Umbrella 1984.

Cohen, Arthur A., Gunnar Kaldewey's New York. New York, Print Collector's Newsletter 1979.

Kaldewey, Gunnar, Über die Herstellung des Buches »New York 1977«. Hamburg, Philobiblon 1979.

Index

Impressum

Graphic Design
Saskia Rothfischer

Photography
Mark Merrett, Averill Park, NY
Getty Center, Santa Monica, CA
Kaldewey Press, Poestenkill, NY

Printed by
Dr. Cantz'sche Druckerei
Ostfildern

© 1997 Kaldewey Press, Cantz Verlag and the authors
© 1997 for works reproduced by the artists and their legal successors

Published by Cantz Verlag
D 73760 Ostfildern-Ruit
Senefelderstrasse 12
Tel. (0)7 11 - 44 05 - 0
Fax (0)7 11 - 44 05 - 2 55

ISBN 3-89322-322-3

Distribution in the U.S.A.
DAP, Distributed Art Publishers
155 Avenue of the Americas
Second Floor
New York, N.Y. 10013
Tel. 212 - 672 19 99
Fax 212 - 672 94 84

Printed in Germany